The Handbook
of
Competency Mapping

The Handbook of Competency Mapping

Understanding, Designing and Implementing Competency Models in Organizations

Second Edition

Seema Sanghi

SAGE | Response Business Books

www.sagepublications.com

Los Angeles • London • New Delhi • Singapore • Washington DC

First published in 2007 by

SAGE Response
B1/I-1 Mohan Cooperative Industrial Area
Mathura Road, New Delhi 110 044, India

SAGE Publications Inc
2455 Teller Road
Thousand Oaks, California 91320, USA

SAGE Publications Ltd
1 Oliver's Yard, 55 City Road
London EC1Y 1SP, United Kingdom

SAGE Publications Asia-Pacific Pte Ltd
33 Pekin Street
#02-01 Far East Square
Singapore 048763

Tenth Printing 2012

Published by Vivek Mehra for SAGE Publications India Pvt Ltd, typeset in 10.5/12.6 pt CG Times by Innovative Processors, New Delhi and printed at Chaman Enterprises, New Delhi.

Library of Congress Cataloging-in-Publication Data

Sanghi, Seema, 1961–
    The handbook of competency mapping: understanding, designing and implementing competency models in organizations/Seema Sanghi.—2nd ed.
        p. cm.
    Includes bibliographical references and index.
    1. Core competencies. 2. Organizational effectiveness. 3. Strategic planning. 4. Management. 5. Employees—Training of. I. Title.

HD30.28.S266   658.4'012—dc22   2007   2007040868

ISBN: 978-0-7619-3598-8 (Pb)   978-81-7829-761-3 (India-Pb)

The SAGE Team: Leela Kirloskar, Koel Mishra, and Rajib Chatterjee

To,
Pradeep, Prateek and Sakshi

Contents

- Networking 193 • Partnership 193 • People Development 194
- Team working 194
● Experiential Sharing
  - Case in Point—One: Hindustan Sanitaryware & Industries
  Ltd.—An Experience 194 • Case in Point—Two: HPCL—
  An Experience 196 • Case in Point—Three: GHCL—An
  Experience 206 • Competency Model 208

List of Tables

List of Figures

List of Boxes

Preface

FTER having devoted a couple of years to the study of competency mapping and consultancy, I observed that both management and managers are keen to develop a competency framework in their organization but have little or no idea of what needs to be done. Though few organizations have a competency-based human resource system, most of the public and private-sector organizations are striving to implement it. I also realized that they are keen to do so but are apprehensive about the current available paradigms. Borrowing the available models might not be very effective—sooner or later one's own model has to be developed. Thus, the idea to work on this handbook was born. The purpose was to write a book which will serve as a guide for both the management and managers striving to develop a competency framework and map competencies and experiential sharing through case studies.

The text focuses on how to develop and map competencies, and design competency models. It is designed to help the management and executives in an organization understand the complexities and dynamics of competency models and related decision making. It will help managers to design and implement the appropriate competency framework. It will also help management students understand the application and know-how of competency mapping, which is primarily to develop the capacity to act, implement, and bring performance improvement in the workplace.

How Does Someone Use This Book?

Part One of the book is divided into seven chapters. At first it is important to understand what competencies are all about. Once this is developed, the next step is to understand the 'what', 'why' and 'how' of developing competency models. Management of change is complex and therefore comprehending the dynamic issues related to developing a competency framework is necessary. This book discusses various competency frameworks to help understand these issues. These need to be integrated with the human resource system. Once the strategic issues are dealt with, the formation of a competency framework is the next action. But how should it be done and what needs to be done? This is explained in Chapter Five, wherein various possible sources of information have been provided. The next step is to map these competencies in an assessment centre. In the first year, resistance is bound to occur and thus the recommendations given in Chapter Seven will be helpful in the course of implementation. Most of the chapters are illustrated with figures and tables along with examples for better understanding. A glossary of Jobs Task Analysis will be helpful in job analysis, which is one of the most important tasks in developing competency models.

In This Edition

In Chapter One, business strategy, environmental imperatives and the changing role of HR as a strategic partner has been added, widening the horizon with an understanding of business, thereby leading to the formation of a customized HR strategy.

Chapter Four is supported by two cases in point with templates; one of a manufacturing organization and another of telecommunication, show-casing the kind of information that may be available in an organization.

Chapter Six has further elaboration on assessment centres in the UK, USA and in the industry.

The special feature of this new edition is Part Two, which is the outcome of research and consultancy assignments taken during the first edition. The Generic Competency Models for Leadership, HR and Competency Model for the automobile industry will give an insight to the user while developing a customized model for their organization. The live examples of Hindustan Sanitaryware Industries Limited (HSIL), Hindustan Petroleum Corporation Limited (HPCL) and Gujarat Heavy Chemicals Limited (GHCL), along with the respective models, individual reports of competency mapping and potential mapping, will be very helpful for all reader in corporate, academic and consultancy sectors.

Seema Sanghi

Acknowledgements

HAVING worked on this book, I can say that no individual possesses all the competencies required to write a book on competencies. However, this work is an attempt to comprehensively address the issues in and around competency mapping. In the development of this text, direct and indirect contributions of several individuals stand out. The first edition was very well accepted; however, readers specially from the corporate sector wanted me to share my experience with various organizations for deeper insight into the subject.

I am grateful to my readers and corporate managers, who gave me feedback from time to time and helped me come out with this edition.

I owe special gratitude to my husband, Pradeep and our children, Prateek and Sakshi, whose patience and support was instrumental in accomplishing this task.

I also acknowledge my staff whose diligent efforts made this work possible.

Finally, I would like to acknowledge the efforts of the team at Response Books who were involved in publishing this book.

Seema Sanghi

PART ONE

PART ONE

CHAPTER ONE

Introduction to Competency

AT the heart of any successful activity lies a competence or a skill. In today's competitive world it is becoming particularly important to build on the competitive activities of business. There has been much thinking about business strategy over the last three decades, particularly regarding what competencies a business needs to have in order to compete in a specific environment. Top management has been identifying corporate core competencies and has been working to establish them throughout the organization. Human Resource Development (HRD) builds competency-based models that drive business results.

What are strategies? According to Jauch and Glueck (1984) 'Strategy is a unified, comprehensive and integrated plan that relates the strategic advantages of the firm to the challenges of the environment. It is designed to ensure that the basic objectives of the enterprise are achieved through proper execution by the organization. Businesses have strategies, a formal planning cycle, a mechanism is devised to devote the resources to it in the competitive environment.' According to Porter (1982) 'Every firm competing in an industry has a competitive strategy, whether explicit or implicit. The strategy may have been developed explicitly through a planning process or it may have evolved through the activities of the various functional departments of the firm.'

There was a time when an organization had a long-term and short-term strategy. The term would be five, 10, 15 years, but today it has shrunk to a year or two. What are the reasons and the forces behind this?

Realities are changing fast. Instead of seeking to create new markets where managers can occupy the competitive advantage by simply being the first ones to get there, they have become too preoccupied with their competitors for existing markets. Competition is to maximize the arena for sharing future opportunities. Organizations, that possess inherent strengths that are core competencies, are likely to have an edge over others. The issues to be addressed are:

- Is it possible to fit neatly the future opportunities within the existing SBU boundaries?
- Is it possible to spread across a number of business units, competencies needed to access the new opportunities?
- What is the investment and time required to build the required competencies?
- Is it possible to bring together and harmonize widely disparate technologies, varying capabilities, diversity in work roles and job demands, stretched out targets, standards and fast changing process?

The answer to all these is in building competencies for an organizational future. Organizations need:

- A conceptual framework for performance measurement, and management system.
- Effective internal and external communications for successful performance measurement.
- To assign clarity and understanding in accountability for better results.
- Performance management systems for decision-making and not just compilation of data.
- Performance measurement to be linked for compensation, rewards and recognition.
- To share the results and commitments openly with the employees.
- Combine the competency-based interventions into the perspective.

Today the business environmental imperatives have made business dynamic (Table 1.1).

Table 1.1: Environmental Imperatives

- Impact of globalization
- Business has taken ownership for performance
- Regulatory mechanisms and converging industries
- Increased sensitivity to shareholder values
- Demand side and competition
- New models of business growth
- Fast changing technologies
- Communication channels
- IT services and IT enabled services
- Value-based management
- Growth opportunities
- Increased operational efficiency and effectiveness with technology support
- On and off shore delivery from/to third world economies
- Focus on competency building

HR strategy is derived from the corporate objectives, goals and broad competitive strategies adopted by an organization. Organizations have realized the need and importance of human beings as an asset. Managers know that their success lies in effective management of HR. In any business strategy, people are more critical than the plan. Strategies can only be effectively implemented if organizations have a competent force of employees. During the past decades, the HR has also evolved and has a more strategic function than ever before (Fig. 1.1).

As the environmental imperatives are playing an important role in redefining the role of HR the challenge of tuning with the environment is increasing. An efficient HR strategy will give direction and bring in change in an orderly fashion. This will include retention, more competent employees, change and conflict resolution, allocation of human resources for the right fit, major business changes affecting human resources, linking the HR process to the mission and goals of an organization and HR functions emerging as a cost or a profit centre.

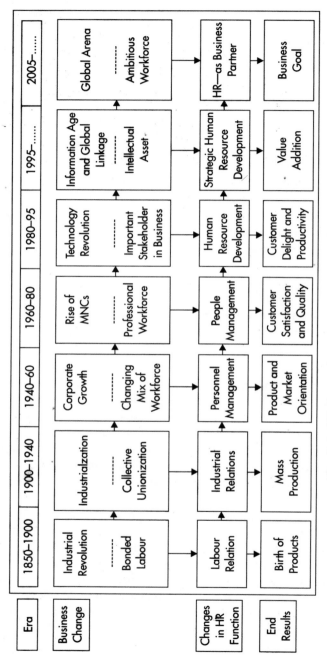

Fig. 1.1: HR Becoming a More Strategic Function

Era	1850–1900	1900–1940	1940–60	1960–80	1980–95	1995–......	2005–......
Business Change	Industrial Revolution / Bonded Labour	Industrialization / Collective Unionization	Corporate Growth / Changing Mix of Workforce	Rise of MNCs / Professional Workforce	Technology Revolution / Important Stakeholder in Business	Information Age and Global Linkage / Intellectual Asset	Global Arena / Ambitious Workforce
Changes in HR Function	Labour Relation	Industrial Relations	Personnel Management	People Management	Human Resource Development	Strategic Human Resource Development	HR—as Business Partner
End Results	Birth of Products	Mass Production	Product and Market Orientation	Customer Satisfaction and Quality	Customer Delight and Productivity	Value Addition	Business Goal

The HR strategy will evolve around building the HR vision and objectives, leading to an action plan through effective and optimal utilization of organizational resources integrated with business processes in order to provide a competitive edge to the organization (see Fig. 1.2).

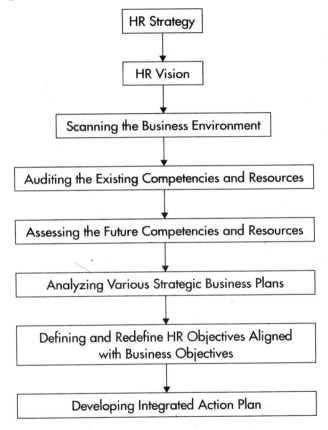

Fig. 1.2: Strategy Linked Action Plan

HR functions today are facing challenges never faced before:

- The areas where the rules of competition are yet to be written are unstructured.

- Senior management has a different way of thinking about the strategy.
- Attaching value to capabilities.
- Risk is involved in managing the realization of value.

All organizations are talking about competencies. Some have truly worked the concept into several of their processes. A few have a fully implemented competency modelling and reporting system in place. These address the development of people from process design through succession. However, quite a few organizations are still striving to build a competency model and implement it. Most organizations, of all sizes, are still struggling with defining, designing and implementing competency model projects.

The process is completely customizable. The decisions of competency design are driven by a number of organizational factors, including management philosophy, customer requirements, business needs, and in-place processes. These factors vary from one organization to another, requiring a customized approach to competencies in the workplace. Customization is essential to the overall success of competency efforts, since every organization must integrate competency concepts into its own job design, recruitment, hiring orientation, development and succession processes.

What is Competency?

Is 'competence' and competency the same?

Some dictionaries may present them interchangeably, however, as shown in Fig. 1.3, 'competence' means a skill and the standard of performance reached, while 'competency' refers to the behaviour by which it is achieved. In other words, one describes what people can

Competence	Competency
Skill-based ⟶	Behaviour-based
Standard attained	Manner of behaviour
What is measured ⟵	How the standard is achieved

Fig. 1.3: The Interface between Competence and Competency

do while the other focuses on how they do it. Therefore there is an interface between the two, i.e., the competent application of a skill is likely to make one act in a competent manner and vice versa.

The plural of each word, therefore, gives two different meanings—competences and competencies are not the same. Competences refers to the range of skills which are satisfactorily performed, while competencies refers to the behaviour adopted in competent performance.

The driving test analogy is useful to understand learning and development at three separate levels.

1. Knowledge—reading (one understands the meaning of driving a car)
2. Skill—practising (one is shown how to drive a car and is allowed to practise in a non-traffic area)
3. Competence—applying (one exhibits an ability to drive in traffic)

There are various definitions of competency but most of them refer to competence. Hogg (1993) defined competency as 'competencies are the characteristics of a manager that lead to the demonstration of skills and abilities, which result in effective performance within an occupational area. Competency also embodies the capacity to transfer skills and abilities from one area to another.'

An analysis of the definition reveals:

- Competencies are the characteristics of a manager. This goes along with our promise that competency is a characteristic of a person.
- Competencies lead to the demonstration of skills and abilities. Therefore, competency must be demonstrated and hence must be observable. It must not be inferred or extrapolated.
- Competencies must lead to effective performance. This means that the performance of a person with competency must be significantly better than that of a person without it. Competency thus refers to behaviour, differentiating success from merely doing the job.
- Competency also embodies the capacity to transfer skills and abilities from one area to another. A sales person may be able to deliver his sales pitch flawlessly but may be tongue-tied

elsewhere. He lacks the competency of communication. Thus competencies cannot be restricted to a single job alone but the person must be able to carry them along. This dispels the need to differentiate between generic and functional competencies since this part of the definition excludes functional competence, which is associated with a particular job.

Another relevant definition, widely accepted among human resources specialists in the corporate environments, is 'an underlying characteristic of a person which results in effective and/or superior performance on the job' (Klemp 1980). A more detailed definition synthesized from the suggestions of several hundred experts in human resources development who attended a conference on the subject of competencies in Johannesburg in 1995, is 'a cluster of related knowledge, skills and attitudes that affects a major part of one's job (a role or responsibility), that correlates with performance on the job, that can be measured against well-accepted standards and that can be improved via training and development' (Parry 1996).

Spencer and Spencer (1993) in their work *Competence at Work* have defined competency as 'an underlying characteristic of an individual that is casually related to criterion-referenced effecting and/or superior performance in a job situation'.

An 'underlying characteristic' means the competence is a fairly deep and enduring part of a person's personality and can predict behaviour in a wide variety of situations and job tasks. 'Casually related' means that it causes or predicts behaviour and performance. 'Criterion-referenced' means that the competency actually predicts who does something well or poorly, as measured on a specific criterion or standard.

There are five types of competency characteristics.

- Motives—The things a person consistently thinks about or wants and that which causes action. Motives 'drive, direct or select' behaviour towards certain actions or goals and away from others.
- Traits—Physical characteristics and consistent responses to situations or information.
- Self-concept—A person's attitudes, values or self-image.
- Knowledge—Information a person has in specific content areas.
- Skill—The ability to perform a certain physical or mental task.

As illustrated in Fig. 1.4, knowledge and skill competencies tend to be visible and relatively 'on the surface' characteristics of people. Self-concept, trait and motive competencies are more hidden, 'deeper' and central to personality.

Surface knowledge and skill competencies (Fig. 1.5) are relatively easy to develop; training is the most effective way to secure these employee abilities. Core motive and trait competencies at the base of the personality iceberg are more difficult to assess and develop; it is most cost effective to select these characteristics.

Competencies can be defined as skills, areas of knowledge, attitudes and abilities that distinguish high performers. These are

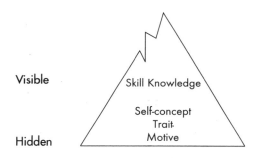

Fig. 1.4: The Iceberg Model

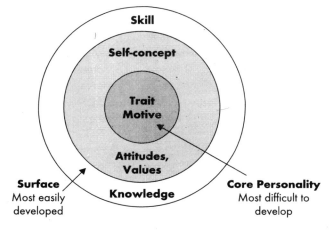

Fig. 1.5: Central and Surface Competencies

characteristics that may not be easily observable but rather exist 'under the surface'—behavioural questions can help draw out examples of these competencies (see Fig. 1.6).

Fig. 1.6: What are Competencies?

Competencies are components of a job which are reflected in behaviour that are observable in a workplace. The common elements most frequently mentioned are knowledge, skills, abilities, aptitudes, personal suitability behaviour and impact on performance at work. There are various definitions with little difference in them. However, the common denomination is 'observable behaviour' in the work-place. The criteria of competency are superior performance and effective performance. Only some competencies can predict performance. Thus competencies can be divided into two categories.

- Threshold competencies—These are the essential characteristics that everyone in the job needs to be minimally effective, but this does not distinguish superior from average performers.
- Differentiating competencies—These factors distinguish superior from average performers.

Gary Hamel and C.K. Prahalad (1994) in their book *Competing for the Future* wrote, 'core competencies transcend any single business event within the organization'. Certain projects are so massive and persuasive that no individual can possess the competencies required to see them through to completion. Therefore, organizations have to identify, develop and manage organizational core competencies that drive large enterprise critical projects. Workplace competencies focus on individuals instead of the organization, and they vary by job positions versus enterprise endeavours. The unit of measure is people rather than the business. There may be core competencies that appear in every competency model position, most workplace competencies are typically specific to the position. Thus there is an enormous amount of work to set up organization-wide competency-based applications. 'Competent' is when a person is qualified to perform to a requisite standard of the processes of a job. 'Competence' on the other hand means the condition or state of being competent.

The difference between the core and workplace competencies is given in Table 1.2.

Table 1.2: Core Competencies vs. Workplace Competencies

	Core	*Workplace*
Scope	Organization	Individual
Purpose	Strategic	Tactical
Participant(s)	Business unit	Worker
Tasks	Processes	Activities
Competencies	Global	Position

Competencies for Competitive Advantage

Philips Selgnick, in his book *Leadership in Administration*, was one of the first writers to acknowledge that factors internal to an organization, such as its personnel and its previous experiences, are crucial to its chances of success in executing a chosen policy. In essence in the field of business activity, the past determines the present. Selgnick said that an organization's developmental history results in its having special limitations and capabilities—a character or emergent institutional pattern that decisively affects the competence of an organization to frame and execute derived policies. He called the peculiar character of an organization its distinctive competence. The art of good management is the ability to make a practical assessment of an organization's suitability to its task or strategy. For instance the management of a boat-building firm specializing in high quality craftsmanship decided to expand into mass production of low-cost speedboats. It proved impossible to adapt worker attitudes away from their historical commitment to quality and craftsmanship. Management was obliged to relocate the speedboat production and recruit a separate workforce. The new venture failed because the history and culture of the organization did not match with the new task. Thus a distinctive competence in one area—quality craftsmanship—may amount to a distinctive incompetence in another sector which adequately has low-cost production. Strategy formulation and opportunity surveillance are useless exercises unless the company has the internal abilities to execute its decision, or at least possesses the chance of developing the required capabilities. Competence, both generic and specific, plays an important role in the success of an organization.

The competence mapped should be linked to the corporate strategy. Igor Ansoff in his book *Corporate Strategy* advocated that managers compile a comprehensive checklist of their firm's skills and resources, that is, a grid of competencies. Similar grids were to be compiled on competitors already operating in a given market. This document became a permanent reference guide for future strategy decisions and could be used in assessing the likely success of diversification.

However, Robert Hayes (1985) criticized what he called the ends-ways-means approach to strategy planning. He questioned whether managers should decide on a strategy before deciding on the means of implementing that strategy. He advised managers not to develop plans and then seek capabilities, instead they should build capabilities and then encourage the development of plans for using this as an opportunity.

Whether it is corporate strategy or internal competencies, mapping competencies is most important and has to be related to the corporate strategy.

More often than not, competencies are an organization's most important resources because they are valuable, rare and difficult to initiate. Organizations can capitalize on this resource—managers, after identifying them, can make decisions about how to exploit them and also learn how to expand them.

Myths about Competency

Competence is not performance but is a state of being, a qualification to perform. It is, in relation to performance, a necessary but not sufficient condition. Workers cannot perform to standards without competencies. But competencies cannot guarantee that workers will perform adequately. Sometimes, extremely competent workers may fail on the job due to a variety of personal or environmental factors. Those lacking competencies can make up for a lot of shortcomings with exceptionally hard work. Competence has to be there but it cannot guarantee results, nor can its absence always predict failure. Competency measurement should not be confused with performance measurement. Competencies are all about being qualified to do the work in a particular position. Performance, on the other hand, is the result of the actual work. A blend of these two activities may cause confusion and eventually disaster. The organizations, by mixing them up, may end up doing a poor job of both competency assessment and performance management which is detrimental to the entire organization.

As shown in Fig. 1.7, it is critical to keep a competency management system separate from a performance management system.

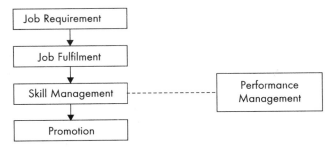

Fig. 1.7: Competency Management System

Competence is not process input—The classic four M's of Total Quality Management as shown in Fig. 1.8, have nothing to do with a worker's qualification to do a job. They are resources that are used to complete the process. Herein, manpower denotes the number of people required to perform the process, not their capabilities; materials, methods and machinery are part of the process as designed. These are resources used by the people to complete the process. Thus they are tools, not competence.

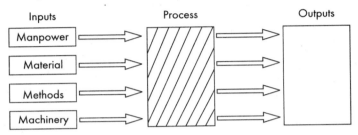

Fig. 1.8: Input Process Output Model

Competence is not process output—Outputs are the business results of a process. They are productive outcomes of competent workers. Results are not competencies. Process results are just one of the many measures of competence. It is easy to mistake outputs for competence because competence is closely related to output. But these are cause and effect relationships, not equilencies.

Competence is not a trait—A trait is a distinguishing characteristic of personality. Personality traits are formed at an early age and it is believed that certain elements of personality may be genetically determined. Even with the help of a trained therapist it is hard to change personality. Traits end up being what someone brings to the job. Once people are on the job, typical development activities have little chance of changing personality. It is said 'hire for traits, train for skills and fire for attitudes'. Traits are attributes such as kind, obedient, reverent, timid, thrifty and courteous. However, traits that have creeped into the competency model are openness, team oriented, empathy, achievement oriented, problem solving, etc. Each competency should be defined by what it means. Competency projects deal with performance issues only. Consequently, traits have no place in a competency model.

Competence is not capability or ability—Capability is a workplace capacity. It connotes potential future performance. Ability is a reflection of talent, of being able to perform. Neither of them guarantees performance. One may have sales ability, administrative ability, one may be capable of taking independent action or capable of resolving problems on his/her own.

The competency process should consider not what workers can potentially do or what talents they could have, if they choose to use them, but what workers actually need, to be qualified to do. Thus capabilities and abilities are not part of the model.

Competence is not a motivational attitude—Motivational attitudes are integral to the personality of a worker, such as aggression, self-confidence, decisiveness, ambition, commitment. Do not make the mistake of including motivational elements while defining competence.

A popular performance analysis tool that allows this approach is the Can Do/Will Do chart (see Fig. 1.9). 'Can do' refers to the employees' qualification to do the job. 'Will do' refers to the employees' motivation to perform as given by Kenneth Carlton Cooper (2000). This results in four possible alternatives as shown in Fig. 1.9.

Cannot Do	Can Do	
Train	Motivate	Will Do
Job in Jeopardy	Counsel	Won't Do

Fig. 1.9: Can Do/Will Do Evaluation Chart

- Can Do/Will Do. This is the ideal situation. The employee is fully qualified and is doing the job as designed.
- Cannot Do/Will Do. Here, the employee is putting in the effort, but is not getting the results (skills problem).
- Can Do/Won't Do—Here the employee possesses the competencies to do the work but does not complete work processes as designed (a motivational problem).

- Cannot Do/Won't Do—This employee has deficiencies in both skills and motivation. A decision has to be made regarding the development/counselling resources required versus the expected success of the effort. The result may well be a job-in-jeopardy situation.

The 'Can Do-Can't Do' dimension of this model is certainly within the purview of a competence effort. But the 'Will Do-Won't Do' dimension is not competency based. It is a matter of motivational attitude. Attitudes cannot be developed, only counselled. Therefore, they cannot be part of a definition of competence.

A Quick Glance at the History of Competency

In the last century business has come full circle in its attitude towards workplace competencies. In the beginning of the 20th century, work brought complex skills to the job. Typical business processes required specific competencies for the task at hand. These competencies could be acquired only through years of on-the-job learning and practise.

Then came the era of scientific management where Frederick Taylor's and Henry Ford's use of assembly line shifted competencies from workers to time-and-motion study. Complexity was minimized and efficiency was maximized with the philosophy and in a depression economy, employees had little value. Process expertise left little scope for training. If the worker could not handle the monotony—boredom, physical strain—a large number of applicants were available to fill openings.

Later, in mid-century, World War II enforced management-centric views where officers gave orders to subordinates who obeyed the commands without questions. Thus somebody had to run things and only those in command were assumed to have the information, perspective and abilities to make decisions.

After the war they still lived under a command and control hierarchy. The task broken into smaller tasks, was done by specialists. In the post-war decade the demand was unparalleled and competition was little. The turnaround came when in the early 1960s. McClelland wrote a landmark article in the *American Psychologist* asserting that IQ and personality tests that were then in common use, were predictors of competency. He felt that companies should hire based upon competencies rather than IQ scores only.

Later McClelland, founder of McBer, a consulting company, was asked by the US Foreign Service (USIA) to develop new methods that could predict human performance. The objective was to eliminate the potential biases of traditional intelligence and aptitude testing. This was the beginning of the field of competence measurement.

The next step was for competency concepts to find their way into mainstream business practices.

McClelland (1973) began by asking the USIA's personnel director and some top managers, for the names of their most outstanding employees. He also asked for the names of people whose jobs were secure but who were in no way outstanding.

To differentiate between the two groups, McClelland and his colleague asked 50 people to describe three incidents where they felt they had outstanding performance and where they felt they had really messed up. To establish a clear picture minute details were asked for—what was said, what was done, when and where it all happened, who else was there and so on. These detailed descriptions enabled them to find out a pattern of what competencies the outstanding performers had demonstrated which others had not.

Many of the skills that the panel of experts had identified as crucial to job performance turned out to be irrelevant to the everyday duties of the people interviewed by McClelland.

In order to validate the conclusions about which competencies were necessary, McClelland tested them on another group of officers who had been identified as outstanding and a group who fell into the mediocre category. Using psychological tests for the key competencies, he found that the officers identified as outstanding consistently performed very well on such tests, whereas those rated mediocre performed poorly. Thus it was clear that the key competencies identified were indeed relevant to job performance.

Chapter Two

Developing Competency Models

THE key to gaining a competitive edge is the ability of the workforce of an organization to maximize the advantages of state-of-the-art technology, superior products, and steady source of capital to enter into the marketplace. A company's technological tools are only as useful as its employer's ability to employ them; they are perceived in terms of how effectively the benefits are communicated (McLagan 1989).

Determining whether the workforce possesses the abilities critical for its success is indeed difficult. Behaviours necessary for effective performance vary from business to business and role to role. Many organizations have thus developed competency models to help them identify the essential knowledge, skills and attributes needed for successful performance in a job aligned with the strategy and integrating it to the HR strategy (see Fig. 2.1).

A competency model describes the combination of knowledge, skills and characteristics needed to effectively perform a role in an organization and is used as a human resource tool for selection, training and development, appraisal and succession planning. Identifying and mapping these competencies is rather complex. Skills can range from highly concrete proficiencies like the ability to operate a particular machine or to write a sentence, to far less tangible capabilities such as the ability to think strategically or to influence others. See, for example, a competency model for sales associates in an organization (Table 2.1).

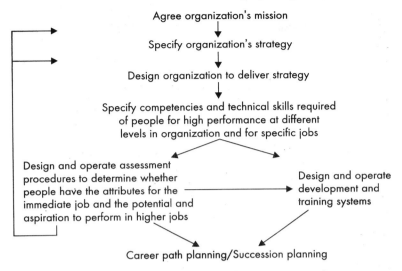

Fig. 2.1: Linking HR Processes to Organizational Strategy

A banking company launched a new scheme of private banking and realized that for its growth it had to develop its sales force. It needed a rapid increase in the number of sales associates. The sales force was needed not only to sell the new product but also address high turnover in field offices and wide variance in sales effectiveness among officers. Thus a sales competency model was developed (Table 2.1), clarifying the characteristics required to succeed in the job. It had an objective: To integrate into the company's selection system on the job, the same criteria for hiring people, as required for effective performance. It was incorporated into the performance management system to ensure that sales people would receive coaching and feedback on the behaviours and skills that had strong correlation to success on the job. The focus was to increase productivity and check turnover.

Knowledge can be either highly tangible and measurable—do you know how to create web pages, knowledge of various languages, or complex matters like do you understand the transcultural issues when operating in the Middle East, or the European financial market. A job needs both, depending upon the degree of concreteness.

Table 2.1: Competency Model for Sales Associates

Personality

Assertiveness	Ability to take command during face-to-face situations while displaying appropriate tact and diplomacy.
Competitiveness	Desire to win and to achieve and surpass goals.
Self-sufficiency	Ability to work independently and maintain one's motivation.
High Emotional Stamina	Ability to maintain focus and effectiveness under stressful and frustrating situations.
High Energy Level	Ability to establish and maintain a fast pace and tempo.

Ability

Mental Ability	Ability to deal with multiple issues and details, alertness and learning capacity.
Divergent Thinking	Ability to see and think beyond the obvious and formulate original solutions.
Quantitative Reasoning	Ability to reason with, analyze and draw conclusions from members.

Knowledge

Financial Analysis	Understanding the financial impact of decisions on the customer, the customer's satisfaction and the company.
Computer Literacy	Basic computer skills for application to marketing programmes, including prospects list, computer contacts and relevant economic data.
Product Knowledge	Expertise related to company's product and services, as well as other crucial aspects of the business.
Competitive Environment	Knowledge of competitive force and how the company stacks up against competitors and their products.

Skills

Basic Selling Skills	Establishing rapport, determining customer needs, relating benefits to product features, handling objectives and closing.
Problem-solving Skills	Anticipating problem-inviting ideas, distinguishing symptoms from causes, modifying proposals and implementing solutions.

(contd.)

Table 2.1 (*contd.*)

Presentation Skills	Ability to communicate to large and small groups, establish rapport with the group, articulate delivery of ideas, read group cues, effectively use vital aids and maintain a commanding presence.
Coaching/Training Skills	Assessing learning needs and closing knowledge gaps, simplifying information, ensuring understanding, reinforcing desired behaviour and motivating the learner.

Attributes or characteristics of the person are most complex and most difficult to measure. Aptitude, reasons and inclination suggests a potential to acquire a particular skill or knowledge. Traits such as extroversion, self-sufficiency and tenacity may indicate a disposition for dealing with certain types of situations or performing certain roles.

A competency model includes both innate and acquired aspects. It is essentially a pyramid (see Fig. 2.2) built on the foundation of inherent talents, incorporating the types of skills and knowledge that can be acquired through learning effort and experience. At the top of the pyramid is a specific set of behaviours that are the manifestation of all innate and acquired abilities.

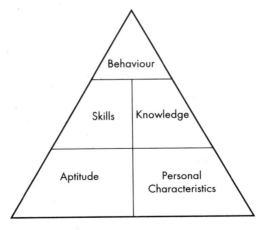

Fig. 2.2: Competency Pyramid Model

For a competency model to be useful as a human resource tool:

- Competencies must be defined along with examples to illustrate when a particular competency is being demonstrated.
- Although the innate characteristics are fixed in a person for the most part, behaviours can be modified and taught.

Thus the data collection process for the development of competency models—which may consist of interviews, questionnaires or focus groups—focuses on concrete specific behaviour that can be taught or altered through training, coaching and other developmental approaches. The observation of outstanding performers helps in validating the behaviour stated in the model, accurately describing the way these individuals carry out work.

Depending upon the objectives, some models are meant to identify the core competencies that are relevant and necessary to all members of an organization, no matter what their level or role. 'Core competencies' refer to behaviours illustrated by all levels of the workforce rather than a business's unique strengths as they are sometimes understood. For example, when a core competency customer focus is to be demonstrated it would be:

Entry-level Customer	Answering a telephone call by the third ring, using polite service representative language, etc.
Regional Manager	Resolving customer problems by coordinating cross-organizational resources, analysing buying patterns to ensure availability of products, etc.

When developing a competency model, keep the following in mind:

- Certain competencies as customer focus might be generic across several organizations, but the behaviour relating to those competencies can still vary widely from one organization to another.

- Within the same organization two management jobs may present very different challenges and require very different skills.
- In order to be as useful as possible, the competency model should be developed with a specific role in mind. Thus even the best off-the-shelf generic competency model, based on very high quality research, will be more effective if it has been customized.

What business needs are addressed in the competency models?

- What skills, knowledge and characteristics are required to do the job?
- What behaviour has the most direct impact on performance and success in the job?

The HRM systems are ensured by a competency model:

Selection Systems	All interviews are looking for the same set of abilities and characteristics.
Training and Development	It provides a list of behaviours and skills that must be developed to maintain satisfactory levels of performance.
Succession Planning	It focuses on the same set of attributes and skills relevant to success on the positions under consideration.
Performance Management	It clarifies what is expected from the individuals.
Appraisal System	It focuses on specific behaviour, offering a road map for recognition, reward and possible advancement.

Further, a competency model helps in ensuring that consistent standards are applied worldwide in a global company.

Hiring the Best Available People

Competency models are a highly useful tool to make sure that human resource systems facilitate and support a company's strategic objectives. It increases the likelihood of placing the right people into the right jobs. Robert Joy of Colgate explains that his company tracks the success of the competency-based selection process by looking at the number of high potential employees in each business unit. 'We track our global high potentials, for example, if we have hired x number of people, we track them on the basis of how well they are performing. At the decision level, we look at succession planning to see how many of the people we have hired fall into the high potential box' (McIlvaine 1998). According to Joy, the process has succeeded in helping the organization locate top talent worldwide.

Productivity Maximization

To maintain the same or higher productivity, it is essential that people have the specific skills, knowledge and characteristics required to be effective. By identifying relevant skill gaps, competency models help to ensure that the training and development budget will be spent wisely. Competency models also allow for the development of appraisal systems that evaluate people on their use of behaviours and practices that directly contribute to competitiveness, encouraging both the business and the individual to focus on whatever will have the greatest impact.

Enhancing the 360-degree Feedback Process

The 360-degree Feedback Process is being increasingly used in organizations for development, appraisal and compensation purposes. It involves a collection of perceptions about an individual's behaviour and its impact on bosses, colleagues, subordinates as well as internal and external customers. Competency models help to ensure that such feedback relates specifically to the competencies crucial to individual or organizational success.

Adapting to Change

Competency models provide a tool for determining exactly what skills are required to meet the different needs of the present and the probable needs of the future. For example, general agents of a life insurance company are responsible for managing the overall operation of the agency. With increased competition the focus shifted to strategic marketing, territory development and building leadership teams. The company was concerned that the people it was selecting to fill the agent's role might not be able to meet the challenges of the changing business environment. By using a competency model to determine what behaviours the general agents were now required to perform, the company realized that the job was very different from what it had been five years earlier. Consequently, the company could begin to adjust its selection criteria to reflect the changing demands of the role. It could also ascertain the training needs of the current general agents by identifying their skill gaps and deciding which of those gaps ought to be addressed immediately to ensure high performance.

Aligning Behaviour with Organizational Strategies and Values

A competency model can be an effective way of communicating to the workforce the values of the senior management and what people should focus on in their own behaviour. For example, a competency-based appraisal system helps to distinguish individuals with the characteristics that are required to build and maintain an organization's values (teamwork, respect for individual innovation or initiative) from those who do not exhibit the behaviours that will support these values. In this way competency models can translate general messages about needed strategy and culture change into specifics.

Over the years many different methods of developing competency models have evolved but all of them follow McClelland's lead of determining what leads to superior performance, identifying top performers and finding out what they do. There are two principles that are followed in these models:

1. Focus on the superior performers without making an assumption.
2. Focus on what they do to perform the given role.

There are various developed models that are used as a basis for selection, training, promotion and other issues related to human resources.

Various Models

- Job Competence Assessment Method—This is developed using interviews and observations of outstanding and average performers to determine the competencies that differentiate between them in critical incidents (Dubois 1993).
- Modified Job Competence Assessment Method—This also identifies such behavioural differences, but to reduce costs, interviewees provide a written account of critical incidents (ibid.).
- Generic Model Overlay Method—Organizations purchase an off-the-shelf generic competency model for a specific role or function (ibid.).
- Customized Generic Model Method—Organizations use a tentative list of competencies that are identified internally to aid in their selection of a generic model and then validate it with the input of outstanding and average performers (ibid.).
- Flexible Job Competency Model Method—This seeks to identify the competencies that will be required to perform effectively under different conditions in the future (ibid.).
- Systems Method—This demands reflecting on not only what exemplary performers do now, or what they do overall, but also behaviours that may be important in the future (Linkage, Inc. 1997).
- Accelerated Competency Systems Method—This places the focus on the competencies that specifically support the production of output, such as an organization's products, services or information (ibid.).

As we see, there are several approaches with solid underpinnings from which to choose. The process used to develop a model must be straightforward and easy to implement. The final product must have immediate practical application, commitment and buy-in for those who will be expected to implement or change their behaviour based on it. The development process should include a step to ensure that the behaviours described in the model correlate with effectiveness on the job.

Development of the Personal Competency Framework

In 1986 the first version of the Job Competences Survey (JCS) was produced in the fields of assessment centres and management competencies in the 1970s and 1980s (Dulewicz and Fletcher 1982; Fletcher and Dulewicz 1984). It was originally used as a questionnaire for the first stage of the job analysis process, for identifying competencies of senior and middle managers in large companies such as Shell International, Barclays, British Gas and Smiths Industries.

The JCS was first conducted in 1988 during the general and senior management courses in the executive development workshop at Hevley Management College. Much of the extensive research which underpins the Personal Competence Framework (PCF) was conducted on those managers. The feedback gathered from the personal discussions in the workshop and additional competencies elicited the PCF. It consists of 45 competencies as shown in Tables 2.2, 2.3 and 2.4. This framework was the basis for developing a generic competency model for Maruti Udyog Ltd.

The Personal Competency Framework

The Personal Competency Framework stems from the findings of the JCS. It consists of 45 competencies under six main headings as shown in Table 2.2.

When rating the appraisees against these competencies, specific scales are employed. The scale used by all raters for assessing performance is shown in Table 2.3.

Table 2.2: The 45 Competencies

Intellectual	Personal	Communication	Interpersonal	Leadership	Result Oriented
1. Information Collection	13. Adaptability	21. Reading	26. Impact	32. Organizing	38. Risk Taking
2. Problem Analysis	14. Independence	22. Written Communication	27. Persuasiveness	33. Empowering	39. Decisiveness
3. Numerical Interpretation	15. Integrity	23. Listening	28. Sensitivity	34. Appraising	40. Business Sense
4. Judgement	16. Stress Tolerance	24. Oral Expression	29. Flexibility	35. Motivating Others	41. Energy
5. Critical Faculty	17. Resilience	25. Oral Presentation	30. Ascendancy	36. Developing Others	42. Concern for Excellence
6. Creativity	18. Detail Consciousness		31. Negotiating	37. Leading	43. Tenacity
7. Planning	19. Self-management				44. Initiative
8. Perspective	20. Change Oriented				45. Customer-oriented
9. Organizational Awareness					
10. External Awareness					
11. Learning Oriented					
12. Technical Expertise					

Table 2.3: Performance Rating Scale

5 Outstanding performance on this competency far exceeds acceptable standards.	2 Performance on this competency is not quite up to acceptable standards. A development need.
4 Very good performance on this competency, better than acceptable standards.	1 Performance on this competency fails to meet acceptable standards. A major development need.
3 Quite acceptable performance on this competency, meets requirements.	0 Unable to rate this competency.

The scale used by the appraisee and employer for rating importance is shown in Table 2.4.

Table 2.4: Importance Rating Scale

5 This behaviour is of vital importance to a successful, overall performance of the job.	2 This behaviour is of highly marginal relevance to the overall successful performance.
4 This behaviour is definitely important to successful performance overall.	1 This behaviour is not relevant to overall successful performance.
3 This behaviour is relevant but not important to the overall successful performance.	

The employer uses this scale for a second time when rating the importance of each competency for the level or type of job the appraisee is likely to hold in three years' time.

The Lancaster Model of Managerial Competencies

The Lancaster Model of Managerial Competencies is a universal management competency framework, developed by Burgoyne and Stuart (1976) and first published in *Personnel Review*, used with permission of authors.

The 11 qualities separated into three groups, as shown in Fig. 2.3, represent three different levels. The first level forms the foundation level, and comprises of two kinds of basic knowledge and information a manager may need to use in decision making and action taking.

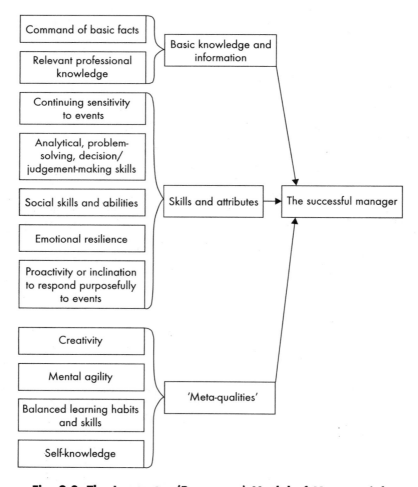

Fig. 2.3: The Lancaster (Burgoyne) Model of Managerial Competencies

Source: Burgoyne and Stuart (1976), used with permission of the authors.

Level One

Competence One: Command of Basic Facts

This competency states that a successful manager should understand the business and have a sound knowledge of basic facts surrounding the business such as short- and long-term goals, product knowledge, and the roles and relationships between various departments.

Competence Two: Relevant Professional Knowledge

This includes knowledge of a specification such as legislation, management techniques, sources of finance or knowledge of basic background management principles including planning, organizing and controlling.

The second category comprises specific skills and attributes that directly affect behaviour and performance.

Level Two

Competence One: Continuing Sensitivity to Events

This means the manager is aware of what is going on and is perceptive and open to information: hard information such as figures and facts and soft information such as feelings of other people. As a result, a successful manager is able to respond in a suitable manner to situations as they arise.

Competence Two: Analytical, Problem-solving and Decision-making Skills

A manager must make many decisions—sometimes these can be made using logical, optimizing techniques. At other times it means using the ability to weigh the pros and cons in what is a very uncertain or ambiguous situation, calling for a high level of judgement or even intuition. Consequently, the manager must develop judgement-making skills.

Competence Three: Social Skills and Abilities

Burgoyne and Stuart (1976) describe interpersonal skills as 'one of the key features of the manager's job'. A successful manager needs to develop a range of skills such as communicating, delegating, negotiating, resolving conflict, persuading, using and responding to authority and power, all of which are essential to interpersonal activities.

Competence Four: Emotional Resilience

This is the ability to deal with the emotional stress and strain that arises as a consequence of working in situations of authority, leadership, power, targets and deadlines. Burgoyne and Stuart (1976) talk about being resilient in coping with this stress. They explain: 'Resilient means, that when feeling stressed, we don't get thick skinned and insensitive but manage to cope by maintaining self-control and by "giving" to some extent.'

Competence Five: Proactivity or Inclination to Respond Purposefully to Events

At times managers must respond to the needs of the instant situation, but whilst making such a response, the successful manager considers the longer-term aims and goals and the impact of the immediate decision. This competence also includes abilities such as dedication and commitment, having a sense of mission and taking responsibility.

The third category consists of qualities that allow a manager to develop and deploy the skills and resources outlined in the second category. The authors have called this third category 'meta-qualities' because 'they allow the manager to develop the situation-specific skills needed in particular circumstances' (Burgoyne and Stuart 1976).

Level Three

Competence One: Creativity

This is the ability to come up with unique ideas or solutions, and to have the insight to take up useful ideas—either your own ideas or ideas from another source.

Competence Two: Mental Agility

This competence is concerned with being able to grasp problems quickly, to think about several things at once, to understand the whole situation quickly and to 'think on one's feet'. 'Given the hectic nature of managerial work these are particularly necessary qualities for success,' explain Burgoyne and Stuart (1976).

Competence Three: Balanced Learning Habits and Skills

Successful managèrs according to Burgoyne et al. exhibit independence as learners rather than depending on an authority figure capable of abstract thinking. Such managers have the ability to use a range of learning processes including use of inputs like teaching, discovery from one's personal experiences and reflection, a process of analysing and reorganizing pre-existing experiences.

Competence Five: Self-knowledge

The final competence concerns the extent to which managers are aware of their own beliefs, goals, values, feelings, behaviour and the part they play in influencing their actions. 'The successful manager therefore needs skills of introspection,' explain Burgoyne and Stuart (1976).

Transcultural Managerial Competencies

The Managerial Competency Mapping Test has been developed to map competencies. This model was used during the selection of candidates for the management course. Another study was conducted with the objective of redefining and ranking competencies to reflect the current business environment. The study was conducted on 308 managers of UK as well as those of Asian origin based in France, Germany, Spain, England and India. The respondents were asked to rate how important and relevant the competencies included in both Burgoyne's and Trompennar's frameworks have been in their development as transcultural managers. Table 2.5 shows the average rating and ranking of various competencies.

Table 2.5: Average Rating and Ranking of Various Competencies

Rank	Competency	Average Rating
1	Continuing sensitivity to events	9.4
2	Social skills and abilities	8.8
3	Awareness of cultural differences	8.7
4	Understanding the importance of relationships	8.2
5	Value and respect for cultural differences	8.0
6	Analytical, problem-solving and decision-making skills	7.6
6	Comprehending emotional expression	7.6
7	Relevant professional knowledge	7.5
8	Emotional resilience	7.4
8	Reconciling individualism vs. communitarianism	7.4
9	Understanding how status is accorded	7.1
10	Mental agility	7.05
11	Command of basic facts	6.8
11	Creativity	6.8
12	Balanced learning habits and skills	6.7
13	Proactively and purposefully responding to events	6.5
14	A desire to reconcile different perspectives into a new and more effective style	6.1
15	Self-knowledge	6.0
16	Reconciling how people relate to nature	5.8
17	Integrating the values of rule making and exception finding	5.6

Continuing sensitivity to events, social skills and abilities, awareness of cultural differences, understanding the importance of relationships, value and respect for cultural differences emerged as elite competencies that were deemed to be vital to achieving transcultural management excellence by current transcultural managers.

Personal Competency Framework—Maruti Udyog Ltd

The Personal Competency Framework was used to identify genuine competencies for various levels for Maruti Udyog Ltd. The project team included key position holders in Maruti in the human resources department, along with the author as the consultant and team leader. The following were identified as competencies for various levels (see Table 2.6).

Planning to Develop a Competency Model

Like any other development work, a foundation has to be laid in order to develop a model.

1. Determine the objectives and scope—Why are we doing it? What jobs, functions or business units will we target? What method will we use to develop the model? Who will carry out the work?

   (a) It is important to identify the business need or needs that are to be addressed. This will help in ensuring the continuous support for the project. Second, it will help the efforts of all participants to remain focused on the objective. Also, it may add to selection, training and development, performance appraisal, succession planning, compensation, etc. It should also address issues of attracting top talent, retaining key employees, ensuring that skills are available to meet the future challenges, aligning cross-organizational teams to get products to the market faster and also aligning people's behaviour with organizational values and strategy.

   (b) The objective and scope of the model needs to be focused on the targeted jobs, functions or business units, increase productivity or instil a specific company value. A competency model is most meaningful if it provides behavioural examples of identified competencies.

   (c) While determining the objective and scope, it is essential to determine the method for developing the competency model. There can be two general approaches:

   • Starting from scratch
   • Starting with a validated competency model

   If the objective is to develop a model for any job, function or role in the organization, then starting from scratch is an appropriate approach. Here, data has to be internally collected from interviews with incumbent and informed

Table 2.6: Competencies for Maruti Udyog Ltd

Level 10	Level 11	Level 13	Managers	IDPM
Competencies	Competencies	Competencies	Competencies	Competencies
Information collection	Information collection	Information collection	Stress tolerance	Stress tolerance
Problem analysis	Problem analysis	Problem analysis	Change oriented	Change oriented
Judgement	Judgement	Numerical interpretation	Written communication	Written communication
Organizational awareness	Organizational awareness	Creativity	Listening	Listening
Learning oriented	Learning oriented	Planning	Persuasiveness	Persuasiveness
Adaptability	Adaptability	Perspective	Ascendancy	Ascendancy
Independence	Independence	Adaptability	Negotiating	Negotiating
Listening	Listening	Independence	Organizing	Organizing
Sensitivity	Sensitivity	Written communication	Empowering	Empowering
Flexibility	Flexibility	Initiative	Appraising	Appraising
Decisiveness	Decisiveness	Energy	Motivating others	Motivating others
Energy	Energy	Customer oriented	Leading	Developing others
Tenacity	Tenacity		Risk taking	Leading
Initiative	Initiative		Business sense	Risk taking
			Concern for others	Business sense
			Initiative	Concern for excellence
			Customer-oriented	Initiative
				Customer-oriented

observers, focus groups and through on-the-job observations. This data must then be analysed to identify the competencies that are significant to effective performance. Though this is time consuming, it focuses on role- and company-specific competencies.

Another approach is when organizations use a validated model as the starting point instead of extensive interviews and observations of incumbents on the job, thus saving time. But such a generic model may not be role or company specific. It is best suited for managerial and leadership roles that cut across functions and positions.

(d) The project of developing a model should be assigned to a team of five to nine people depending upon the scope. The team should comprise of individuals who are responsible for implementing and using the model, key stakeholders, one or two individuals with experience and practice in competency model development and a visible sponsor who can act as its advocate within the organization.

2. Clarify implementation goals and standards—What is the intended result of the project? How will we know when we have achieved it? To provide direction to the project the goal should be expressed in terms of performance or output. The goal should be specific, realistic, attainable, challenging, consistent with the available resources and the organization's policies and procedures, measurable and should have a deadline. To develop an excellent model, the implementation standards should address quality, quantity and timing. This should include a set of standards to identify what actions must be taken to meet them.

3. An action plan is essential—What are the tasks that are involved? Who is responsible for carrying them out? When must they be completed? What are the resources that are required? An action plan is essential to manage the workload, review and monitor the progress of the project and communicate it to the team members. Another integral part is to identify the possible problems and be ready with a contingency plan to address those issues. An action plan should comprise of action steps broken into work that needs to be done, and deliverables into tasks and

activities; accountabilities for carrying out each step; schedule specifying the set start, completion dates and various milestones; and requirement of resources including equipment, people, money, etc.

Certain problems are predictable and others are not. Advance planning for likely impediments will lessen their impact and minimize the impact of any unforeseen event. The problems that arise may be related to time and changed priorities, influence of stakeholders, power and political resources, resistance and skill. There is thus a need to review each step and plan as a whole, raising questions on what could go wrong where, and be ready with a contingency plan.

While developing a contingency plan, one must prioritize the listed potential problems that are most likely to arise in the implementation; determine the probability of each and the seriousness of its impact; assign accountability for these preventive measures; and draw up a list of contingency actions. This exercise would help in changing or modifying the course of action if needed, and provide people outside the project team with step-by-step information about the development process. Outgoing communication on the progress of the project is vital for its success. It helps reduce the likelihood of the project being stalled or derailed.

4. Identification of individual performance against established performance criteria—What does successful performance on the job look like? What job outputs or results will be examined? Against whose performance will the findings be tested? The identification of individuals at various performance levels is necessary when developing a model. First there is a need to determine the successful performance related to job output or results and then to differentiate the behaviour of successful performers from that of those who are less effective. Once the performance criteria are agreed upon, an interviewing and observation pool has to be created in order to identify superior performers, mediocres and those who fall below expectations. Other alternative methods can be performance appraisals, ratings of effectiveness from direct reports and colleagues and inputs from a panel of judges. The quality of the performance criteria

is very important because that would serve as the foundation for many steps and ultimately indicate the success of the model, ensuring that the people whose competencies have been identified have actually demonstrated these by successful performance.

Caution: It is essential to understand the business need which drives the project and identify the key success factors. The competency model should reflect the unique aspects of the position in a given organization and not be developed in a vacuum. However, if for reasons beyond control, the objectives are changed during the development of the competency model it would mean compromising with the usefulness of the model itself. Therefore the application of the model should not lose focus midstream.

CHAPTER THREE

Issues Related to Developing Competency Models

W HENEVER a new thing is decided to be introduced, a number of questions arise. Following the problem-solving approach to decision making, it is of utmost importance to find out what the problem is. Facts need to be gathered in order to establish the problem. Decision making has to be linked with the short-term and long-term objectives. Once the objective is clear, the next step is to generate alternatives. There should be adequate brainstorming while generating alternatives. Sometimes, even the alternative which appears to be insignificant may emerge as the action plan. These alternatives are to be evaluated against the various chosen criteria for the action plan to emerge.

It is an old saying that 'power lies not with those who have all the answers but with those who have the questions'. While building competency-based models, a host of questions occur—the problem is that there is no right or wrong answer. To achieve ultimate effectiveness it is necessary to address all the issues, alternatives, pros and cons.

Is the Organization Serious about it?

Until there is total commitment, the competency model project is sure to be doomed. Most of the organizations have to simply go for it because it is a mandatory requirement to seek ISO certifications or any other national/state quality certification/award. If the employers understand that an ISO certification is necessary to retain certain customers or attract new customers, or that the quality award will help in marketing products or services, the acceptance is complete, from the top to the bottom of the hierarchy. Competency is seen as a potential tool but developing the model is difficult in most cases.

When individuals take actions that are different from what they want to do, the purpose of what they want to achieve is defeated.

- Organizations may have a collection of worthwhile projects which are killed by the managers and supervisors who are supposed to execute them. All efforts of top management to take decisions will fail without their buy-in.
- Organizations where total commitment from top to bottom is not there, and if they neither see the benefits nor have the culture to support the competency philosophy, the process should be stopped.
- The methods of personal decisions should be uniform; if they vary from department to department, organizations may put themselves in a legal risk. Competency-based applications must be universal in the organization.
- Leadership must have a vision to drive the process and the potential to complete it; benefits have to be communicated adopting the various methods from top to bottom.

What is the Goal—Quality or Excellence?

The question is what is the organization trying to accomplish? Is it striving for quality or excellence or both? Quality and excellence are two different terms. Quality is an absolute state—in the control of total quality management, quality is conformance to requirements, doing things according to standards. Excellence is a relative term, to put it simply, it is being better than others. It requires comparison. So it can be said that quality is built in, while excellence is designed. If the goal is quality, it means individuals will be assessed on whether they meet the established standards. It is assumed that they possess the minimum competencies. If the goal is to achieve excellence, individuals will be assessed on their competence levels based on a continuous evaluation scale. Hence when evaluating for excellence, it would be necessary to compare the relative competence between two employees in addition to measuring their competence against the standards scale.

Is the Development Effort Periodic or Continuous?

The decision depends upon the environment and the industry. If the environment is stable, the competencies would have changed little over the years. But in most organizations, work activities, job responsibilities and personnel assignments are in a constant state of flux. Every change generates new job titles and/or processes requiring adjustment or changes in the position of competency models. Where continuous modelling is required, either the change can be slowed down to keep the models up to date or the change will be driven by customer demands and competitive processes which has its own pace because it is not in the control of the organization. It is important to ensure that the development efforts, whether periodic or continuous, are really genuine. To do so, the management must be willing to provide sufficient development resources periodically and for continuous development it must link development efforts to planned changes or changes that have been anticipated in the near future.

Is the Assessment a Continuous Process or is it a One-time Endeavour?

Should the assessment be periodic or on demand? The determining factor is when the assessment is scheduled. If the annual assessment plan is decided for the entire year, a batch assessment process must be completed. If it is being continuously monitored, a continuous assessment application can be created. The administration of an assessment is also a major factor. Traditionally, the assessment and reporting of the group is done at once. Forms are distributed and collected; responses are collected and recorded. Nowadays, competency assessment and reporting can be completed over the intranet within the organization at any time for all positions. It is continuously updated with the individual assessment results. Computerization, however, depends upon the expert application designer, voluntary or mandatory assessment process and the maturity of a competency assessment model. Initially, to start with it is useful to have a batch approach. Every individual is assessed at once, and group results are immediately available for validation. The larger the group, the more valid is the sample study. The value of assessment, irrespective of the approach, lies in the accuracy of the model and validity of the assessment tool/instrument.

Are the Competencies Reflecting Current Activities or Future Activities?

The issue is deciding whether the model reflects what the situation is or what it should be. Continuous quality improvement or re-engineering the process are continuously evaluated and incrementally improved by the organization or it results in temporary periods of radical change. This creates a significant challenge in developing a competency model. If the processes are broken, continuous change can be monitored periodically but if the processes are locked, it can become a massive impediment to change. Existing appraisal systems should cover the experiment. The question that arises is: who is sufficiently qualified to assess employees on something they are not yet doing? How would the standards be set? How do new processes drive competency needs and how do available employee competencies drive process options? How does one develop, identify and assess anticipated competencies for new processes? The quality improvement team and the competency project team should form a team to analyse relatively stable processes and accept the continuous responsibility of the model. .

What should be the Time Frame for the Project?

Usually the management and managers, because of inexperience, feel that like any other activity, a competency model has a classic start and completion date. But actually, competency is a successive application and the relative mature state can be reached only with stable processes. In the first year, the stress should be on the development of the model and initial assessment. The second year should show a refinement in the model and assessment, with improved results. The managers will then have more familiarity with the process through growth in the comfort level. A comparative assessment of the current year and previous year helps in new development activities and creates needs that are to be utilized.

By the third year it should reach a certain level of maturity. The focus here is on the maintenance rather than development. In some cases there might be immediate benefits in the first year, but dissatisfaction is also a possibility and weaker areas need to be addressed. There is a need to make the commitment stay on for multiple rounds, until the desired results are obtained.

How will the Organization Use the Results?

Competency models and their application usually create a certain fear and scepticism. The management of change is not easy. Leadership questions how to make use of it in alignment with the organization's strategy. The employees' perception is to raise questions regarding the interests of the management. The management or employees' competency effort is an illusion. If the attitude is 'this is yet another innovation of human resources which shall meet its fate ... the effort shall be doomed'. The results may be used for downsizing, promotions or selections, etc. Competency assessment will rank the employees, indicate future needs, determine whether positive business results were generated or raise skills that target learning and development activities. The end result will be used for the development of the employees to succeed or be used as a punitive measure. The higher the level of trust between the management and employees, the higher would be the willingness to be candid and accurate in assessment. The competency assessment process should be kept separate from the performance management process. As long as the competency assessment process is linked to human resource applications, even if it is used only for development purposes, employees will always be sceptical. Thus it is very important to keep them separate; gradually when the model matures it may be integrated, as the trust level would be much higher.

What is the Value Addition for the Organization?

What the organization desires, is the classic question. There may be various desired outcomes.

* Requirement of quality certification programme for staying in business.
* Enhancing organization's stature and competitive position.
* Improved recruitment and selection processes.
* Right people in the right jobs internally.
* Developing people in time and according to the needs.
* Better performance and the dropping of unnecessary development activities by focusing on the need of the job.
* Overall organizational performance by capturing market share, improved customer service, innovation, improved efficiency, decrease in time to market and better decisions.

The message has to be reinforced by repeating that the management really means it.

What is the Value Addition for Employees?

If the message is communicated that the management 'really means it', results are positively going to add value for the employees.

* Clarity of processes, skills and knowledge required to meet the established standards.
* Knowledge about where employees meet required qualifications, thus not wasting time in unnecessary development activities.
* Determine competencies for the jobs that an employee aspires for.
* Rationalizing personnel decisions by promoting truly qualified employees and allowing others to take advantage of set standards to become qualified.
* Increase in competency levels and improved working conditions, thus benefiting both the individual and the organization.

- More opportunities in the form of new positions and available promotions with the growth of the organization.
- Availability of information to determine job qualifications and to fill in employees' gaps.
- Shift from formerly subjective personnel process to management by fact.

How will the Determinants of Success be Measured?

It is most important to measure the determinants of success if it has to be managed. If it is training, the team should establish what and how much was done other than effectiveness.

- There can be an internal quality implementation member versus an external quality certified lead auditor to identify what went well, what should be included and what needs to be stopped.
- Judgements can be based on how the project compares with the benchmark experiences of other organizations.
- The determinants of business results like reduction in turnover costs, decrease in programming errors, faster time to market, customer satisfaction, profitability, etc.

All this requires measurement of current performance at the time of starting the project than at the time of implementation.

What are the Desired Outcomes?

The desired outcomes can be the following deliverables:

- Competency Model—Generic competency model for the organization as a whole along with a specific competency model for specific positions.
- Position standards for each competency and for each job.
- Measurement instruments/jobs to determine levels of competency.

- Gaps identified between employee's competence and position standards.
- Linking results with the enrolment database and with position curriculum.
- Career development plan.
- Training calendar.
- Training need analysis by identifying the gaps observed and adding them to the course schedule.

The focus should be on highlighting what the organization wants to be able to do.

Who is the Owner of the Process?

Every process should be owned by somebody who is responsible for the overall success and continuous enhancement. Is this the responsibility of HR? Ideally, it should involve individuals from various departments excluding those whose appraisal will be adversely affected by the outcomes of the project. Line managers and workers are essential in creating and evaluating competencies and assessment instruments. Whosoever is responsible for the project will have the authority to own the process. The owner should be centrally located with the experiences of HR process and training. There are logical conditions for ownership.

Who All will be Targeted?

A generic competency model comprises core competencies which are not too specific, which cannot be a substitute for individual positions. Therefore to being with, the process can be started from a single department but ideally the following needs to be present:

- Scope to develop competency models for jobs at various levels representing different kinds of work activities.
- Commitment from the leader with efforts to enthusiastically support the managers, supervisors and frontline employees.

- Departments/Divisions with a positive and healthy climate and without any hidden agenda or leadership dysfunctions would be ideal for the project.

A competency model should be developed for relatively structured job positions and duties rather than for a department that has extremely complex interdependent jobs. The pilot programme should aim to establish organizational processes on competencies.

Who All will be Involved in Development?

All the stakeholders and at least one person who is not affected by the process should be involved in the development of the model. The team should be able to perform job analysis, and develop tools and instruments for assessment. They should have the background for interviewing, survey, questionnaire development and statistical analysis. There is no substitute for knowledge and skill. The team can be from within, depending upon qualified professionals and hired consultants or they can be outsourced. A realistic team would consist of members from within along with a professional consultant.

Who will be Assessed and by Whom?

For any assessment, the basic requirement is the validity and reliability of the assessment instruments. Are the instruments valid to measure the competencies needed to drive the desired business results? Are they reliable to accurately capture the competency levels of employees? There are various methods of assessment, indicating who is assessed and by whom.

- Bottoms-in-seats Assessment—This is a curriculum-based assessment wherein training curricula are developed by position. Employees present in the training are measured for the competence. However, it does not ensure any level of competence. The modules should be standardized along with the methods. This method of assessment has a minimal level of functionality and reliability.

- Self-assessment—One of the classical methods is self-rating on the competencies by administering assessment instruments. This is welcomed as employees best know their needs. The question that arises is whether employees are qualified to assess themselves. It is assumed that employees possess the knowledge and ability to assess themselves. But for organizations aiming at quality certification, if the individuals were qualified to assess themselves there would be no need of any certification. Individuals may not have the experience to rate themselves on various competencies in the overall organizational perspective. Each one would rate themselves depending upon their own understanding, varying from superior employees to not-so-superior employees. Understanding of each and every word is essential for both generic and specific competency models, or else there will be a problem of consistency. As the assessment will be linked to HR processes, employees may be reluctant to report the assessment accurately because of a motivational bias. This is more likely to happen when the assessment is linked to promotion opportunities. Another major problem is the perceptional bias. Some individuals cannot judge themselves accurately. They may either overestimate their competencies or underestimate their competencies. In either situation, the results are derailed.

In spite of being a convenient and intuitive method, it is not very reliable.

- 360-degree Assessment—This refers to round-the-circle complete feedback; performance is appraised by superiors, subordinates, peers and customers. This is a better gauge of an individual's competence. Feedback on personal competencies (abilities, skills and personal characteristics) is a vital foundation upon which an individual can build and develop himself/herself. Some salient features of the 360-degree Assessment are:

  o Team approach eliminates blind spots on the basis of self-assessment.
  o Team synergy makes better decisions than individuals.
  o Difference between self-assessment and team assessment can be readily measured.

o Self-analysis is useful; group analysis is more valid.
o Difference between self-perception and group perception can be compared.
o However, the concern about the qualification of employees to assess competencies is multiplied. Subordinates, peers and even superiors may have less knowledge about the jobs of others. Therefore, the question of validity arises.
o What is the level of interaction between the co-workers?
o Have they actually done the job?
o Do they have an understanding of the process?
o Are they trained to assess?
o Are they internally consistent in their own ratings and also externally consistent with other respondents in assessing individual co-workers for various positions?

The problem of motivational bias arises because the co-workers who are assessing may be competitors for upcoming promotions. This calls for a clash of personal interests. Perceptual biases are reflected in assessing co-workers. They do not really assess competencies but is an indication of how satisfied he or she is with the co-worker on various competencies. If not monitored and managed carefully and continuously, he/she may become a battle zone, shooting anonymous shots.

A number of common constraints or problems have been documented in research regarding the use of the 360-degree appraisal in numerous organizations around the world (refer to Clifford and Bennett 1997). Some of the more critical potential stumbling blocks are listed below.

Problems may arise if:

• The purpose of the process is not clearly communicated and understood by the appraisee.
• The wrong instrument has been chosen for the appraisee's job.
• Appraisees feel threatened by the process and results (33 per cent of the 800 organizations surveyed in a study identified this as the main obstacle).
• There is a reluctance on the part of the appraisee to invite peers and subordinates to give ratings. The possibility of reprisals, vendettas and vindictiveness is a major concern.

- There is a lack of concern for the highly sensitive data which needs careful feedback.
- There is a similar lack of concern for anonymity and confidentiality.
- The true meaning of the result becomes clouded by prejudice, politics or sycophancy.

Business Results—The emphasis here is on individual results and not on group or departmental results. It links the individual and his competence with the desired business outcomes. But if it becomes a flawed assumption, when employees do not have control on the complete process, this cannot be solely responsible for outcomes.

The approach discussed focuses on the performance, but competence assessment ascertains the level of competence to do the job and not the performance. However, the competency model is often linked to performance, appraisal and promotions. The best alternative would be to use a range of assessment techniques depending upon the competencies being measured.

How to Validate the Assessments?

- Select the top superior performers and the bottom 10, not average performers, and administer a test. The test should reflect the relative competency levels. Informal verification such as data from the group, interview summaries of the record and comments may be one way to validate the assessment.
- Just after the assessment, a quick survey can be done by openly asking the employees about their opinions regarding the reliability of the assessment. The responses should be kept confidential and should be anonymous. The analysis should be done by an outsider.
- To check the accuracy, a sample of employees from all levels can use the assessment instrument. The differences can be worked out through discussions until an agreement is reached.
- The 360-degree feedback can be used for validation. The respondents can specify the responses.
- A sample of respondents can be contacted to verify every item of assessment at all levels. The data should help the

standardization so that true assessment can be determined. Statistical analysis would identify the percentage of responses where the ratings were higher or lower than the actual.

- Several of these techniques can be utilized concurrently. Each technique would make a unique contribution, which would be an abiding block at the first stage. Usefulness may range from involvement, by understanding the model and its administration, to generating quality data and facilitating improvement in assessment instrument.

How will the Competency Project be Communicated to the Employees?

Communicating any major change which is driven by asking for a certain amount of uncertainty will give way to rumours, fear and anxiety. Expecting people to be welcoming or being enthusiastic is too much. Communicating that the management 'really means it' is essential for success. This should be communicated through all possible formal and informal communication channels. A positive environment has to be created along with transparency of its application in the HR functions. Feedback from all levels, especially frontline employees, will be most helpful.

The important decisions on the competency model project must be made at the start of the project in order to eliminate later problems. Management by all means, should express it 'really means it' by being committed and communicating, funding, supporting and executing the decision. The outcome and its usage must be clear. To achieve success, the implementation should be done right from the start or not be done at all.

CHAPTER FOUR

Competency-based Application

IN 1996, the American Compensation Association (ACA) mailed questionnaires to HR professionals in 19,106 North American companies. Two per cent of these, i.e., 426 were returned. From these, a total of 1,257 competency-based applications were identified, 70 per cent of which were underdeveloped. Table 4.1 shows how long the four types of competency-based applications had been installed. The bulk of applications were in place for less than two years.

Table 4.1: Durations of Competency-based HR Applications

Application	Staffing	Performance Management	Training and Development	Compensation
In development	29%	33%	44%	52%
<1 year	26%	25%	14%	17%
1–2 years	29%	28%	25%	21%
3–5 years	12%	11%	10%	7%
>5 years	3%	3%	7%	2%

The early adopters were implementing competency-based HR applications for a number of potential benefits. Table 4.2 shows how the respondents thought that competency-based HR applications would help their organizations to focus behaviour.

Table 4.2: How Competency-based HR Applications
Focus Behaviour

Factors	Respondents Selecting (%)
Communicate valued behaviour	48
'Raise the bar' of the competency level of all employees	45
Emphasize people (vs. job) capabilities, enabling the organization to gain competitive advantage	42
Encourage cross-functional/team behaviours critical to business success	34
Reinforce new values while continuing to support the achievement of business objectives	27
Close skill gaps	26
Support superior performance in roles/units that have a critical impact on organizational success	22
Focus people on total quality/customer-centred behaviour	22
Provide an integrating vehicle for human resources	20
Ease the flow of people across business and global boundaries	8

The ACA data provides further insight into the effectiveness of competency-based applications. The feedback on 148 models that had been in place for more than a year showed mostly positive experiences, but with a difference in various factors.

Competency-based HR applications focused on behaviour levels. Focus and emphasis was also increased. However, improvements in competency, skills and performance were still too early to tell for many respondents. What was concluded was that the focus must be on developing competency-based processes that drive improvements.

Effectiveness of competency-based HR programmes was different for various factors:

1. On focusing people on total quality/customer-oriented behaviour, the positive effect was 80 per cent, the don't know/

too early to tell group was 20 per cent, no effect was 0 per cent and negative effect was also 0 per cent.

2. On emphasizing on people (vs. job), there was 69 per cent capabilities, enabling the organization to gain competitive advantage. The positive effect was 69 per cent, don't know/too early to tell was 23 per cent, no effect was 4 per cent, negative effect was also 4 per cent.

3. On 'raise the bar' of the competency level of all employees, the positive effect was 59 per cent, don't know/too early to tell was 41 per cent, no effect was 0 per cent and negative effect was also 0 per cent.

4. On close skill gaps, the positive effect was 50 per cent, don't know/too early to tell was 50 per cent, no effect was 0 per cent and negative effect was also 0 per cent.

5. On support of superior performance in roles/units that have a critical impact on organizational success, the positive effect was 30 per cent, don't know/too early too tell was 70 per cent, no effect was 0 per cent and negative effect was also 0 per cent.

The close alignment of competency applications with customer-centred behaviours is apparent and is seen as an immediate result by respondents. They also report a positive effect on competitiveness. But the impact on actual reduction of employee competency levels and the support for superior performance of key individuals and departments is less clear.

The findings have something to do with the overall newness of the competency applications but they may also reflect problems with implementation. The applications evidently got everyone thinking in the right direction but not necessarily performing better.

The concept of competency applies to the full range of HR functions. The role of competency is to move the employee through the organization in a cyclical fashion, from one position to another.

The competency-based HR functions, as illustrated in Fig. 4.1, are as follows:

Position Requirement

Process Design—The process determines what skills and knowledge is needed. The desired outcomes form the basis of a

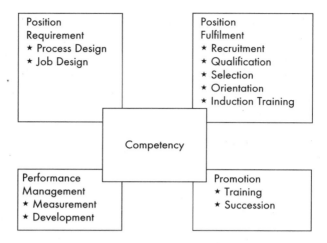

Fig. 4.1: Competency-based HR Applications

measurement system for determining qualifications of workers in the process.

Job Design—Once the qualification and skill on knowledge is determined the task can be assigned to individuals or teams. Job requirements are used to identify employee competency levels and qualifications.

Thus, for a position of an HR manager in an organization one has to look into the Knowledge, Skills and Attitudes (KSA) needed for that particular position. It would require qualification, business results and measurement systems to determine qualification at the individual and team levels as given below:

HR Competence Audit

The following checklist is used to assess the HR competence of the people performing HR functions in the organization as given in Table 4.3.

5: Has this competence in abundance.

4: Has this competence adequately.

3: Has this competence but can develop some more.

2: Needs to develop this competence substantially.

1: Does not have this competence, needs to start developing it.

Table 4.3: HR Competence Audit

HR Knowledge

 1   Knowledge of HR philosophy, policies, practices and systems
 2   Knowledge of performance appraisal system practices
 3   Career planning and development system and practice
 4   Knowledge of organizational diagnoses and interventions
 5   Knowledge of learning theories
 6   Knowledge of training-methods and systems
 7   Knowledge of organizational structures and how they function
 8   Knowledge of group dynamics and group function
 9   Knowledge of links between organizational goals, plans, policies, strategies, structure, technology, systems, people management systems, styles, etc.
10   Knowledge of power dynamics and networking in the organization
11   Organizational plan, manpower and company requirements
12   Knowledge of social violence research methods
13   Knowledge of job analysis, job enrichment, job redesign and job evaluation
14   Manpower planning methods
15   Knowledge of role analysis techniques
16   Knowledge of employee relation practices
17   Knowledge of the role of reward
18   Knowledge of the methodology of behaviour modification and attitude / change
19   Knowledge of quality circles
20   Knowledge of recent development in management systems
21   Knowledge of personality theories and measurement
22   Understanding of personal and managerial effectiveness
23   Knowledge of interpersonal relations and factors affecting them
24   Knowledge of what constitutes an organization's health and methods of survey
25   Knowledge of instruments and measurement of human behaviour
26   Knowledge of personal growth and its methods
27   Knowledge of turnaround strategies
28   Knowledge of creativity and problem-solving techniques
29   Knowledge of conflict management techniques and strategies

(contd.)

Table 4.3 (*contd.*)

HR Skills

1   Influencing (communication, persuasion, assertiveness, inspirational and other skills needed to influence) top management
2   Influencing skills needed to influence line manager
3   Articulating HRD philosophy and values
4   Designing skills for developing HRD systems
5   Communication skills: Written (ability to communicate views, opinions, observations, suggestions, etc. clearly to make an impact)
6   Communication skills: Oral
7   Skills to monitor the implementation of HR systems (designing questionnaires, data gathering, feedback and persuasion)
8   Interpersonal sensitivity
9   Ability to give and receive feedback
10   Counselling skills (listening, rapport building, probing and exploring)
11   Conflict-management skills
12   Ability to inspire others by arousing their values and superordinate goals
13   Leadership and initiatives
14   Creativity
15   Problem-solving skills
16   System designing skills
17   Task analysis/Job analysis skills
18   Organizational diagnosis skills
19   Process observation and process sensitivity skills

Personal Attitudes and Values

1   Empathy and understanding
2   Positive and helpful attitude to others
3   Faith in people and their competencies
4   Introspective attitude
5   Openness (open to others' suggestions and in expressing his or her own views)
6   Interpersonal trust
7   Productivity
8   Respect for others
9   Self-confident; faith in one's own competencies
10   Sense of responsibility

(*contd.*)

Table 4.3 (*contd.*)

11 Sense of fairness (constant desire for objectivity and resistance to being impressionistic)
12 Self-discipline (desire to set examples)
13 Honesty (desire to be sincere and honest)
14 Willingness to experiment
15 Learning orientation
16 Willingness to treat every experience as a learning opportunity
17 Perseverance
18 Work motivation (desire to be involved in and work harder for the organization)
19 Superordination (an attitude that he or she is working for larger goals)
20 Empowering attitude (A tendency to respect others and a willingness to empower them, by not being overly concerned about a personal power base)
21 Stress tolerance (ability to cope with stress, frustration, hostility and suspicion)

Analysis

These three areas—HR professional knowledge, HR skills and personal attitudes and values—are the true depiction of the competency of a HR professional. A 5-point scale ranging from having competency in abundance to having no competence on each element and its scores would indicate where we stand vis-à-vis HR capabilities. 'The competency of a professional is determined through his or her level of knowledge, capacity to utilize skills and personal attitudes and values towards the HR function' (Chanda and Kabra 2000).

Position Fulfilment

- Recruitment—Competencies are the basis to determine who should be interviewed and evaluated along with skills and knowledge. This is a costly and time-consuming effort that can be reduced through proper understanding of what competencies a candidate can bring to the job. The competencies should be well defined so that their meaning is clear and there is no ambiguity.

- Qualification—To determine whether the candidate is qualified to perform the job or can master the requirements of the position, it is necessary to evaluate competency.
- Selection—While selecting an individual, competency assessment is used to determine the best person to fill the position.
- Orientation—This refers to developing the general competencies required of an employee, by the organization.
- Induction Training—This refers to developing the specific competencies where there are gaps, to meet the desired performance standards of the position.

For position fulfilment it is important to have competencies with definitions and ratings. In case the competencies identified are creativity, learning oriented, flexible and analytically skilled, these can be rated on a 5-point scale as stated in Table 4.4.

Table 4.4: Competencies with Definitions and Ratings

Rate the individual on each of the competencies using the 5-point rating scale	Rating Scale	Use this 5-point scale to indicate level of performance
	(1) Exceptional	Consistently exceeds expectations
	(2) Very Good	Consistently meets or exceeds expectations
	(3) Good	Consistently meets expectations
	(4) Satisfactory	Does not meet expectations consistently
	(5) Unsatisfactory	Consistently fails to meet expectations

Competencies	Rating				
Creativity: Produces highly imaginative and innovative ideas and proposals	1	2	3	4	5

(contd.)

Table 4.4 (*contd.*)

which are not obvious to colleagues with lesser perspective.					
Takes Initiative: Proactively initiates changes or takes action towards efficiency, addresses existing and potential problems, satisfies customers and finds new opportunities.	1	2	3	4	5
Learning Oriented: Actively identifies own learning needs and opportunities. Is effective in applying new learning in a work context.	1	2	3	4	5
Exhibits Flexibility: Effectively adapts when faced with changing situations, unexpected pressures and varying job demands.	1	2	3	4	5
Uses Analytical Skills: Uses relevant facts, data and analytical tools to draw accurate and meaningful conclusions.	1	2	3	4	5

Once the competencies are identified, a list of interview questions along with the competency rating sheet is needed to elicit information about relevant behaviour. An interview panel may probe further to get the relevant information, for example as given in Table 4.5.

Table 4.5: Selection Interview Questions

1. Describe an incident in which your workload was too heavy.
2. How did you handle the situation?
3. Tell me about a situation when you were trying to accomplish something and did not have ready access to the necessary resources. How did you get them?
4. Describe a situation in which you had to juggle more than one task. How did you handle them? Which one did you handle first and why?
5. How did you manage your time and task?
6. Tell me about a situation when your planning was not helpful. What happened then and how did you recover?

(contd.)

Table 4.5 (*contd.*)

7. Tell me about a time when you had to deal with two people asking you to work on different projects that required more than 100 per cent of your time. How did you resolve the situation?
8. State an example when you were not able to achieve the goals. What did you do?
9. Describe a situation where your performance was excellent. What were the circumstances? What did you do? How did the people respond?

An interview rating form provides a continuum of unacceptable to acceptable behaviour examples, with three to six behaviour examples of each competency. Interviews may use a structured rating form to bring in objectivity along with focus in the interview, relating to what is the standard that is needed for a position. For listening skills (as given below) the definition of competencies needs to be clearly marked out. The competency is marked on a point scale with an 'above' and 'below' standard. Also given below is some space for the repondent to explain why a certain standard has been chosen. This helps evaluators to focus on the behaviour needed for a particular position without assessing mere feelings. This describes exceptional performance, thus the rating scale is for frequency or effectiveness of competency as given in Box 4.1. However, the rating form states the importance of the competency to current or future role (see Table 4.6).

Performance Management

- Measurement—A people-driven process; it is essential to have measurement of workplace competencies.
- Development—The development activities are relative and are received while on the job. They are designed to support the continuous improvement of workplace competencies.

For performance management it is necessary to have a list of behaviour descriptions for skill improvement along with a checklist of specific behaviour examples (see Box 4.2). A description of three to five levels of effectiveness for each competency is helpful in understanding and assessing the person from above standard to below standard as given in Box 4.3.

Box 4.1: Interview Rating Form

Rate the candidate for each competency (circle one number in each category)

Competency	Above Standard		Meets Standards		Below Standard
	5	4	3	2	1
Listening	Listens dispassionately, is not selective in what has been heard. Conveys the clear impression that key points have been recalled and taken into account.		Listens dispassionately but is selective in what has been heard. Generally conveys the impression that some points have been recalled and taken into account.		Is passionate, selective in what has been heard. Often conveys the impression that the key points have not been recalled and taken into account.
Why?					

(contd.)

Box 4.1 (*contd.*)

	5	4	3	2	1
Developing Others	Makes every effort to develop both on and off the job, the knowledge, skills and competencies of subordinates or others required to advance their career.		Generally puts in effort to develop both on and off the job, the knowledge, skills and competencies of subordinates or others required to advance their career.		Rarely tries to put in effort to develop both on and off the job, the knowledge, skills and competencies of subordinates or others required to advance their career.

Why? _____

_____

_____

_____

Table 4.6: 360-degree Feedback Questionnaire

Please describe how often this manager uses each of the following specific behaviours. Read each statement carefully and mark your answer in the column to the right. For each of the practices, choose one of the following responses:

1   Never, not at all
2   Seldom, to a small extent
3   Sometimes, to a moderate extent
4   Usually, to a great extent
5   Almost always

The five numbered choices refer to how often this person uses this behaviour. Please be as honest, objective and accurate as possible.

This person . . .

1. Gathers information to understand customers' business strategies and their view on market opportunities.	5	4	3	2	1
2. Keeps abreast of new developments and innovations in the customers' markets.	5	4	3	2	1
3. Keeps abreast of emerging trends and initiatives involving the industry's competitors.	5	4	3	2	1
4. Determines how his/her organization's strategic competencies help customers achieve strategic objectives.	5	4	3	2	1
5. Evaluates customer opportunities using a long-term perspective.	5	4	3	2	1
6. Welcomes opportunities to customize product/service offerings to assure they meet customers' long-term needs.	5	4	3	2	1

Promotions lead to succession planning and are based on the performance of individuals. The 360-degree feedback aligned with the competency model is an important component for promotion. This includes the competency description of behaviours and the ability required for the current job, along with the ratings indicating the current level of ability as given in Table 4.6.

Box 4.2: Behaviour Examples

Competency	Description of Behaviour
Developing People	— Assembles strong teams
	— Stretches, empowers and trains people
	— Communicates effectively with people
	— Provides rewards, feedback and recognition
	— Demonstrates and stimulates passion and commitment
Commitment	— Widely trusted
	— Takes ownership
	— Candid and forthcoming
	— Delivers on commitments
Values and Ethics	— Aligns with company values
	— Adheres to code of conduct
	— Rewards right behaviours
	— Ensures that laws are obeyed and safety as well as environmental protection are practised
Vision and Purpose	— Sees possibilities, optimistic
	— Creates and communicates compelling vision or direction
	— Inspires and motivates
	— Aligns the organization
Performance	— Sets and achieves ambitious goals
	— Listens and responds
	— Drives for continuous improvement
	— Measures the right things
	— Gets results
	— Ensures that health, safety and environmental objectives are met and integrated into business activities

Box 4.3: Competencies with a Range of Observable Behaviour on a 5-point Scale

Performance Review Form

General Competencies

Points to consider . . . .
- Ratings should be based on specific behaviour and not impressions.
- Ratings should be based on day-to-day performance not isolated incidents

5 points

5	4	3	Customer Oriented	2	1
Strength Prioritizes internal and external customers' needs, always uses knowledge of the customers to make decisions, gains customer's trust.				*Development Need* Does not prioritize customer needs, seldom uses knowledge of the customers to make decisions, does not gain customer's trust.	

(contd.)

Box 4.3 (contd.)

5	4	3	2	1
		Teamwork		
Strength Initiates and supports meaningful projects, demonstrates trust in team members, serves on teams and celebrates success.			*Development Need* Seldom initiates projects, does not demonstrate trust in team members, does not serve on the team or celebrate success.	
		Problem Solving		
Strength Anticipates problems and identifies their causes before implementing solutions, acknowledges when a plan is not working and takes appropriate steps to fix the problem.			*Development Need* Seldom anticipates problems or identifies their causes before acting, does not act even when it is clear that a plan is not working.	

- Succession planning—Candidate evaluation refers to the information required to adequately plan for a potential candidate's development progress and evaluate readiness as shown in Box 4.4. This is similar to the interview data form that can be used to discuss a candidate's readiness in the most relevant job-related areas. Box 4.4 is a bit detailed. Instead of a range of behavioural examples it includes a place to record development plans, followed by succession planning as given in Box 4.5.

Promotion

- Training—This is a position fulfilment function. The objective is to prepare individuals for new positions before placing them there in order to be immediately productive. Competencies help to determine when the gap is fulfilled and the candidate is ready to move up.
- Succession—There is a strong personal link between both the incoming employee and departing employee. The incoming workers need more than baseline competencies and should be able to take over current projects while least disrupting the processes involved.

Competency Models Can Enhance Human Resource Management (HRM) Systems

An understanding of the full range of HR functions can further be integrated with the HRM systems.

Selection	Includes position requirements, recruitment and selection.
Training and Development	Includes orientation and induction training, training for development, position fulfilment and performance management.
Appraisal	Includes performance measurement for performance management.
Succession Planning	Includes training and succession for promotion.

Box 4.4: Succession Planning Candidate Evaluation Form

Please evaluate the candidate using the 5-point scale and explain the rating in the space provided.

	Below Standard		Meets Standard		Above Standard
	1	2	3	4	5
Emotional Resilience	Not at ease under pressure. Tense. Nervous		Satisfactory composure and effectiveness under pressure		Entirely at ease. Relaxed and poised. Maintains effectiveness under pressure
Why?					
Assertiveness	Submissive. Unable to assert self		Assertive. Moderately forceful		Very assertive. Can rapidly take command of face-to-face situations
Why?					

	1	2	3	4	5
Independent	Overly dependent. Difficulty in functioning on own		Adequately self-reliant		Self-starting. Proactive. Independent

Why? _____

	1	2	3	4	5
Sociability	Cold, aloof, unfriendly. Difficult to relate to		Sufficiently amiable, friendly and pleasant		Exceptionally personable. Enjoys conversation and projects warmth

Why? _____

Box 4.5: Succession Planning

Candidate Evaluation and Development Planning Form

1 = Proven strength
2 = Meets expectations
3 = Needs improvement

Rating

Position	Possible Candidates	Ready When	Business Acumen	Vision and Purpose	Commit-ment	Developing People	Next Step

Competency models can play a vital role in every process of the HRM system (see Box 4.6). The continuity that competency models can bring into the HRM system would certainly benefit an organization. Understanding the value of competency models to various HRM systems is helpful in judging how best to apply them in the organization.

Benefits of Using a Competency-based Selection System

- Provides a complete picture of job requirements—A competency model provides a complete picture of what it takes to perform the work, thus ensuring that interviewers look for characteristics that are needed to do the job well, in addition to required skills and knowledge. It also provides a method to the interviewers to provide candidates with a clear and realistic picture of what will be expected of them.
- Increases the likelihood of hiring people who will succeed— It would be worse to hire a person for a key position who fails to perform effectively. After interviewing a candidate for a couple of minutes or even hours depending upon the position, the employer should be able to determine whether the candidate has the potential to succeed in the job; it should not be based merely on how one happens to write a persuasive resume and make a good first impression. Incorporating a validated competency model into the selection system addresses this problem, identifying the competencies with a strong correlation to high levels of performance on the job (Holdeman et al. 1996). Thereby the interviewers can judge who lacks a critical set of skills, knowledge or characteristics and focus on those with strong potential.
- Minimize investment in people who do not meet expectations— Hiring the wrong person has a tremendous impact on the productivity and profitability of an organization. When such a person leaves either due to poor performance or because he was not the right fit, the time and money spent in hiring and training becomes a waste. Also, replacement efforts have an adverse impact on productivity.

Box 4.6: Format of Competency-based Applications

Application	Format
Position Requirement	— Qualification and skill required — Business results — Measurement systems to determine qualification at individual and team levels
Position Fulfilment	— Competency with definition — List of interview questions to elicit information about relevant behaviour — Interview rating form providing a continuum of unacceptable to acceptable behaviour examples — Three to six behaviour examples for each competency that describes exceptional performance — Rating scale for frequency or effectiveness of competency — Rating scale for importance of the competency to current or future role
Performance Management	— List of workshops or development experiences available for skill improvement — Description of three to five levels of effectiveness for each competency, from above standard to below standard — Checklist with specific behaviour examples for each competency
Promotion	— Competency with description of behaviours/ability required to perform the job — Rating process to indicate current level of ability — Suggestions for how to develop competency

Andrea Eisenberg, with her extensive work with Fortune 500 clients, an expert in the areas of retention and development compares organizations that use competency models for selection with those that do not. 'The optimal investment of human resources dollars happens when we allocate resources to developing those people who will be successful rather than allocating dollars to people without requisite competencies. Money spent to develop people with the right potential has a long-term pay back and is key to retention. My clients who might have resisted the use of competencies initially have enhanced their implementation when they see how a systematic approach to selection using this technique can enhance financial, personal and organizational results' (*Public Communication*, January 1999). Therefore, using a validated competency model to select individuals who have a higher likelihood of meeting expectations can help minimize the time, money and energy spent in selecting and training candidates.

- Ensures a more systematic interview process—Very often, a person's list of accomplishments enhanced with the right chemistry and impression created during the interview, leads to selection decisions. Unfortunately, this is only part of the information that is needed to determine if a candidate will succeed, particularly at the entry level where a candidate has only educational qualifications but no experience.

In a selection interview, the interviewers should be consistent in what they look for and how they determine whether a candidate is right for the job. The competing model ensures that everyone involved in the selection process is working on the same criteria. They must concentrate on job-related factors that are required for success and compare the candidates on the vital job related factors along with candidates' qualifications.

- Helps delineate trainable competencies—Often, interviewers become impressed with a candidate and very few identify gaps in the latter's abilities. It is important to determine whether these gaps can be addressed through training and development.

A competency model answers these questions; it not only clarifies the competencies most relevant to success but it also pinpoints the attributes and capabilities that are easily developed through training and those that are more difficult to develop. Judging the quality and quantity of training that the candidate would require for effective performance would then lead to a decision which is informed and realistic.

Benefits of Using a Competency-based Training and Development System

Using a competency model as the basis of a training and development system helps to avoid a short-term perspective and ensures that the system focuses on the right things rather than the latest things (Davis and Olson 1996–97).

- Enables focus on relevant behaviours and skills—Identifying strengths and weaknesses seems to be straightforward, but methods such as feedback from others, introspection, experience, some kind of testing or a combination of these gives the basis of what an individual is good at and where he needs to improve. Competency models play an important role in keeping people and organizations focused on the skills, knowledge and characteristics that affect job performance. These models can also help people better assess their current capabilities and determine the behaviour they need to develop to improve their effectiveness (Eubanks et al. 1990).
- Ensures alignment of training and development—A competency model provides focus for training and development opportunities and ensures that they are the ones that are essential to the success of the organization. An effective training and development system must take a long-term view of organizational needs, and it must focus on developing the talent that is currently unavailable in the workforce in order to meet these needs. A well-structured competency model includes behaviours with a strong correlation to effectiveness on the job and also those required to support the organization's strategic decisions and

develop as well as maintain the culture needed to achieve its business objectives.

- Makes the most effective use of training and development— Using a competency model helps remove the guesswork of where to focus scarce resources, by differentiating between programmes with the most impact on performance and those with little relevance to behaviours people need on the job. It also helps in determining who needs which skills and at what point in their careers. Thus people receive training and development when they have a use for it, increasing the likelihood that the relevant skills will be applied and reinforced through experience on the job.

- Provides a framework for bosses/coaches—Training and development provides ongoing feedback, identifying the most useful on-the-job development opportunities, reinforcing concepts and techniques learnt in training programmes. The competency model enables bosses and coaches to fulfil this role in a high quality manner. The model ensures that both the boss/coach and the direct report have the same picture of what it takes to succeed in the job, along with examples of behaviour that can be used as the basis for constructive development discussions.

Benefits of a Competency-based Performance Appraisal System

A competency model can address many of the issues related to performance appraisal. This ensures agreement on performance criteria, what is accomplished and what is not accomplished, collecting relevant and sufficient data. It also ensures opportunity to supervisors to observe behaviour, specificity and concreteness in discussions about performance deficiencies and handling of large amounts of data in a structured manner.

- Provides a shared understanding of what will be monitored and measured—A competency model integrated with performance appraisal ensures a balance between what gets done and how it gets done. The concern is not only with results but with the behaviour and manner with which those results are attained. It provides a shared picture of what is considered relevant and important to effective performance. Models aligned with the business objectives specifically outline the performance criteria that will be used to measure effectiveness and success in that position.

- Focuses and facilitates the performance appraisal discussion— Organizations face the challenge of discussing a person's behaviour in a manner that is focused and useful and does not put the individual on the defensive. The skills, knowledge and characteristics that are important to success are clearly described. It provides a roadmap of where to begin the discussion and what areas to focus on.

- Provides focus for gaining information about behaviour—An appraisal process includes a simple, accurate method for a boss to assess job performance. But what happens when the boss is new or he/she controls a number of different locations? By identifying the specific behaviours crucial for effective performance, competency models offer bosses a starting point.

Benefits of Using a Competency-based Succession Planning System

For succession planning there is a need for a list of the positions under consideration, agreement among the decision makers about what is required for success in each position, who is ready and why, who will be ready soon, accompanied by the person's development needs and recommended actions to close the gap. Succession planning integrates the various systems of HRM with the model given below:

HRM System	Elements
Selection	Criteria for successful performance and identification of those people who are most likely to succeed
Training and Development	Clarification of strengths and weaknesses, development, planning skills, training and on-the-job experience

Appraisal System   Monitoring progress, coaching and
                          evaluation

All of them together identify and develop individuals who are
believed to have the potential to fill specific and senior positions.
The competency model adds value to these other systems by
contributing to the effectiveness of the succession planning system.

- Clarifies required skills, knowledge and characteristics—
  Competency model helps to define the abilities that are necessary
  to fill the role and also those behaviours that are strong predictors
  of success. However, it cannot guarantee that the right decision
  will be made.
- Provides a method to assess candidates' readiness—Determining
  if and when candidates are ready for a role requires a method
  to assess their strengths and weaknesses. A competency model
  along with the 360-degree feedback process serves to create an
  agreed-upon list of the criteria required by the job.
- Focuses training and development plans to address missing
  competencies—A competency model and the 360-degree
  feedback process create a powerful pairing to pinpoint the areas
  that require improvement before a candidate can advance in an
  organization. The competency model describes the competencies
  needed in the role and the feedback provides a method of
  assessing a candidate's current competencies.
- Allows an organization to measure its bench strength—A
  competency model allows an organization to assess its bench
  strength. Individual and aggregate assessment of competency
  levels and relevant behaviour can help identify the presence
  and absence of key capabilities at the organizational level.

CHAPTER FIVE

Formation of a Competency Framework

COMPETENCY models are position models which are at the heart of every competency-based HR application. A competency model is a GIGO (garbage in–garbage out) test factory. Inspite of timely administration intricacies and sophistication, if the models are not accurate and do not represent the relative position, the purpose of the model is lost. The basis of generating competency models are processes. Thus the questions that need to be raised are:

- What does the employee have to be able to do?
- What does the employee have to know in order to do it?

If the flow charts of the job processes are laid, determining of competencies is easier. If the competencies are not related to specific process steps then the model is not valid.

Sources of Competency Information

To get started, the project team asks—what do we do? The best way is to follow a top-down approach from general to specific. There will be a category of competencies that have been taken for granted, which may be reason for careful consideration.

- By assumption—Certain competencies are assumed to be present in every employee. These are closely related to conditions of employment addressing behaviour, ethics and work habits. The model expands from this point. Attitude affects the job and correlates to performance. Many teams do not take time to discuss these in the competency models as they are assumed to be traits that every worker possesses. However, it is necessary to consider them as the competency model will ultimately be expanded beyond employee assessment and development in the areas of selection and promotion. These are important for employee acquisition and should be present in the model. For example, honesty is one of the competencies essential for all jobs in supermarkets as they have enormous problems due to delivery personnel and check-in clerks. Many chains require that all employees complete psychological honesty tests before being hired. New employees then attend follow-up training on ethics and business control during their orientation period. On the other hand, someone taking an office job and shifting papers all day may never receive any specific training in ethics. A conscious decision has to be taken by the project team involved in the competency modelling regarding what is going to be utilized throughout the HR process.

- By Law—Government and its associated regulatory agencies create requirements that apply to all workers. These are massive potential sources for competency. This requires not only knowledge of the regulations but also an understanding of how to comply with them and report the results. Regulations also provide a source of position competencies for workers in specific industries. For example, a truck company must follow strict rules for handling hazardous materials. Warehouses have to pass inspections of the physical plant and procedures. The cost for non-compliance can be enormous in terms of health and welfare, actual damages, legal fees and regulatory lines. These massive sets of rules and regulations must ultimately find their way into the competency models for truck company jobs; including administrators, supervisors, loaders and drivers.

- By Industry—Individual industries have their own professional competency models and assessment approaches. These range from licensing to industry group guidelines and certifications. Certification programmes provide an excellent source of general industry competencies.

The following need licensing examination for practitioners:

Insurance sales agents
Professional engineers
Lawyers
Police officers
Firefighters
Nurses, etc.

There are hundreds of industry-wide examples for certification programmes such as:

Certified life underwriter
Certified financial planner
Certified medical representative
Certified stenographer

Also, there are thousands of vendor certification programmes usually for usage, maintenance and repair of products. The study material and sample examination of such certification provide great input to position models and assessment instruments, and can save the development team a significant amount of work.

- By Organization—The vision and mission statement of the organization reflects the overall philosophy of the organization: Where it is headed to, what it does and how it should act? The organizational competencies that employees will bring to their jobs need to reflect the changing mission and vision of the company. These statements can establish an overall theme for the model and also be useful when it comes to establishing the model.
- By Work Group—Departments in many organizations have their own resources of vision and mission statements. They may also have specialized procedures and documentation that apply only in situations unique to their work group. Work-group-level competencies are more common in organizations with hybrid job structures. Everyone in the department may need to be qualified to do anyone's job. Work-group-level competencies

are required when the model is designed to allow multiple titles to be assessed by using the same framework. This database also becomes the basis for career and succession planning or upcoming positions.

- By Background Information—A special category of competency input has to do with background knowledge. This provides whatever general business, industry or company information is required to meet job standards. Project members are forced to rethink about the knowledge and skills that are assumed to be present in all candidates and so are usually omitted from a competency model. This is important particularly when the model is extended to hiring and promotion decisions. They have to decide what information can be included everywhere, what can be excluded in the position model but later included in the hiring/promotion version, and what can be assumed to be present and excluded everywhere. A chemical company offered a series of personnel development courses on an optional sign-up basis. The HR department was surprised to see that only two courses out of the 15 offered had full enrolments— basic maths and basic reading skills—as the fee was quite reasonable. It was noticed that a large number of employees were hired without the minimum skills to do the job.

In another organization, after a two-week orientation process, a saleswoman was to deliver some information to a customer location. It was only when she enquired about the bus route that the manager realized she did not even possess a driving licence. During the hiring process it never occurred to anyone that a person could not drive.

Thus the question arises, what knowledge and skills are we taking for granted or actually overlooking? Are they important for employees to possess and can they be improved? If so, are they worth including in the competency model and assessment approaches?

Position Documentation

Organizations generate a large amount of documents that can be reviewed when developing competency models. Various sources provide material more than the project team would typically examine in depth. While selecting the source the team should look for: What is most complete, what is considered most accurate, what is available and how much time it will take to review? Existing documentation reinforces the current processes. In this competitive environment where changes are rapid, research and feedback documentation is considered to be an available resource for designing new processes.

- Industry Research—Academic journals, publications and periodicals are sources for the most recent developments of the model. Research-based publications have a hypothesis test with a conclusion format. If the conclusions focus on misconceptions, that needs to be correlated. However, if it indicates the best current practices, it provides information about what the new processes could be. No matter what the industry, a rigorous search effort perhaps conducted by third-party experts using library, business indices, trade publications and internet searches can generate excellent results.
- Vendor Information—A resource that is often overlooked is vendor publications. Suppliers must have extensive support materials and processes in place to help buyers install, run and maintain the complex equipment. Such reference material can prove helpful for developing competencies for production jobs. Many suppliers have extensive Research and Development (R&D) operations that issue marketing and reference documents about their industry and products. Frequently asked questions, operating guidelines, productivity tips, etc., can provide tips to identify competencies.
- Customer Feedback—Customer feedback is a very powerful source of information. Customer satisfaction is one of the top measures of quality; customers both internal and external should give an input to the competency model. Satisfaction measurement is another circular process, with customers providing feedback on survey line items and then responses being used to develop competencies and priorities. The limitation of feedback is that customers sometimes do not know what to ask for. The focus is only on how the organization is performing. This can be used as another instance of reinforcing existing competency models at the expense of continuous improvements.

- Regulations—Written regulations and reference materials, while often overwhelming in size or scope, can provide important insights into what competencies employees must bring to the job.
- Certification Requirements—Professional certification programmes are excellent sources for position competencies. Certification standards, assessment processes and study materials highlight skills and knowledge that are required for certifications. Reviewing any relevant industry or professional certification programmes can provide a proven list of potential competencies.
- Quality Programmes—Another source of generic workplace information can be found in quality recognition programmes such as ISO 9000/14000 or any other quality certification. The quality application is a document that helps identify competency requirements. They require a description of key processes and their principal requirements. These provide direct input into competencies. Quality improvement efforts are always excellent sources of competency information because they require organizations to document goals, processes, performances and results.

Process Documentation

Quality revolves around processes. If processes are efficiently designed and have no defect, the organization will be successful. Therefore, process documentation is an important source of competency information.

- Procedure Manuals and Flowcharts—The classic procedure manual is becoming obsolete as it takes too long to document processes that evolve with frequent changes in an organization and changing customer demands. Such procedures locked in writing or embedded into interactive administrative systems are a poor customer satisfaction approach, yet a good source for competency modelling. Flowcharts are excellent resources as they help to quickly identify the knowledge and skills that are required to complete a process. They highlight activities and decision points of a process, whereas value-added flowcharts list process steps to shorten the process cycle time; and to increase customer satisfaction by identifying when no value is being added to the products, paperwork and information system. Steps which add no value are eliminated. Thus, manuals and flowcharts are very useful for documenting competencies for current operations.

- Time Logs—Time logs is an approach used in time management analyses. Developing time logs requires that employees write down everything they have done in a representative workweek, usually in 15-minute increments. This captures everything as a complete list of activities. If time logs are filled completely and accurately they generate an extremely large amount of data to be analysed. Though time consuming, time logs are one of the most accurate, objective ways to document 'what is' for positions.

- Job Task Analysis—A hands-on approach to observe and investigate how people work, what they do, what is being done in a position and then take a conceptual step backwards to identify Job Task Analysis varies depending upon structured and unstructured tasks and work cycle. JTA professionals while performing studies use traditional methods like interviewing or documentation review. While analyzing, the analyst should not become part of the work system. He/she should be experienced enough to detect when employees are tempted to 'game' the observer in order to keep the demands they face as low as possible to get a realistic view of the position. JTA can be an extremely useful and accurate method of developing competencies. Data required for developing JTA can be obtained only as first-hand information. For the process to be successful, there has to be a standardization of approach, methodology and analysis.

Questionnaires may be valuable instruments for gathering data about competencies, which are vital or relevant to successful performance of a job or group of jobs. If there are a number of jobs with the same title across an organization, a questionnaire can be used to gather a large amount of data in a standard format from many people both quickly and inexpensively.

It is valuable to obtain the view of not only the job holders, but also of their bosses, who are likely to have a broader perspective of the job context and of all the interrelationships. In addition to showing those competencies which are relevant, results can also be presented to display competencies on which respondents disagree. Results from generic jobs or single jobs can constitute a valuable starting point for an overview of the key elements and help to focus subsequent discussions. Common methods of job analysis are Critical Incident Techniques as well as the Behavioural Event Interview as developed by Hay McBer, Consultants. Each method has its pros and cons and there is no single way to produce consistent results. One which fulfils the requirements of the situation is the best. The behaviour is divided into three categories—routine, recurrent and practised; and those that are different for the job itself and which produce effective results (details later in the chapter).

Thus there are various techniques of job analysis:

Observation—Employees are observed as they perform a job and information is collected and analyzed. But this is costly and time consuming.

Interviews—Supervisors and job holders are interviewed to ascertain the main purposes of the job, the activities involved and the relationship it entails. Various types of interviews are discussed later in the chapter.

Diaries—Job holders are asked to keep a detailed log of their activities over a period of time. It is more suitable for complex jobs.

Questionnaires—Employees answer a set of questions about the task that they perform. There are several job analysis question-naires available in the market. These inventories of job analysis measure various traits and skills that are essential for various jobs and positions; they include mathematical skills, communication skills, decision-making responsibility and other skills useful in a job.

Critical Incident Techniques—This technique developed by Flanagan (1954) requires observers who are frequently doing the job, such as supervisors, clients, peers or subordinates. Observers are asked to describe incidents of effective and ineffective behaviour of a person over a period of time. There are thus occasions when the job holder did something well or when the performance was poor. This is a particularly effective technique in competency mapping since it gives an idea about the person-oriented characteristics such as those competencies which are needed in a person to perform a job well.

Repertory Grid Techniques—This technique was developed by George Kelly (1955) and is based on his Personal Construct Theory. It is a very useful interview technique which is rather projective in nature. It highlights those behaviours which are associated with effective performance. The advantage of the repertory grid technique is that it can elicit the skills needed to do the job from knowledgeable observers with no constraints placed on the answers given, unlike in questionnaires.

Customer Contact Maps—A common quality tool for studying customer service is to build a customer contact map. This comprises of every instance in which a customer, internal or external, is touched by the organization, department or position as in value-added charts. Contact maps provide a different way of looking at processes—totally customer focused. This may be categorized by face-to-face conversations, inbound and outbound phone calls, mailers, brochures, advertisements, etc. To identify competencies, the question to be asked is 'What do employees need to know or do to be able to satisfy the customers for this particular contact?'

Existing Documentation

Organizations document job requirements and standards in order to legally hire and terminate employees. It represents the current job and addresses positive competencies.

Job Descriptions—Possible competencies can be readily determined from well-written job descriptions. Job descriptions include the following basic information:

- What level of knowledge do employees need to know and how is that skill acquired?
- How should the employees process that knowledge and skill?

- What is the scope of responsibility as far as decisions are concerned?
- What is the flow of interpersonal communication?
- What is the impact on results when the employees make an error?
- What are the control mechanisms to prevent error?
- What confidential and sensitive information is available to the employees?
- What is the scope of financial responsibilities?
- What is the environmental level of stress and exposure on the job?
- How does the employee direct supervision?

All these factors are linked to specific competencies.

Union Contracts—Though not a popular source of competency, they define exactly what a union employee is expected to be able to do; and the rules for what each union position can and cannot do under the current agreement.

Departmental Planning Documents—The goals and projects described in the departmental planning documents have projections such as 'what is to be done for the coming year' which are helpful in a changing environment.

Performance Plans—Performance plans are focused on people-level activities and assignments. They highlight what is expected from each individual employee and at what level each employee is expected to perform. All of them are competency-related issues.

Appraisal Forms—Performance appraisal form is a standardized form used for distinct classes of employees.

Personnel Development Resources

The training and development department is an excellent source of information on competencies. Department activities are targeted at performance enhancement and are already in a competency format ready to be used. Training needs analysis and training programmes that are planned and conducted as also the training calendar are a ready source for information on competencies.

Interviews

Hard information can be attained from data process, procedures, manuals, etc. However, the only source available for competency items on soft skills is interviews, focus groups and customer conversations. The challenge in using these methods is the ability to step away and analyze the competencies required and make a link between participant feedback and competencies. Sorting out and identifying competencies through the heap of data created during interviews is another challenge.

The first challenge in utilizing soft information is maintaining validity and accuracy. The challenge is similar to that of self-assessment. Those involved in a process may not have the professional skill or ability to analyze required competencies. Project team members will have to make the link between participant feedback and competencies.

Another challenge is sorting through the mountain of data that soft information investigation creates. Do you know that at an average speaking speed of 150 words per minute, interviewers generate 6,000 words per hour? That is if we are assuming that they speak two-thirds of the time and the interviewer speaks for the remaining one-third. If 10 workers are interviewed for an hour each, the verbatim results could fill a medium-sized business book. This when multiplied by different jobs across various departments results in the project team having created an encyclopaedia of raw competency data.

Once a large organization brought focus groups together at the beginning of the model building. It was decided that ten position holders would be invited for the department. The groups generated more than two thousand different competency entries for a single department. The project team had to create a specialized database in order to track the entries but inspite of that the data was almost incomprehensible. It took almost three months to sort, analyze and consolidate the process along with long meetings and discussion. Thus it is very important that while collecting soft information steps are taken to obtain enough data to be reliable but not too much so as to overkill.

The best approach is to adopt a minimalist attitude—like McClelland interviewed the top performers and those who were not so satisfactory and asked specific questions related to their success and failures. However, additional interviews or meetings can always be held later to gather more data. As in the example given earlier, the project team could have conducted simple telephone interviews selecting on the basis of past performance with two or three people on each job; later they could have decided whether to apply a multi-focus group approach.

Interviews should be conducted periodically as that generates better results. The feedback should be continuous instead of getting all the data upfront; then showing the competency model and assessment instrument to job holders for a final check right before rollout. Continuous feedback facilitates problem identification and immediate correction during the development phase.

In the development of the model, the job holders are the internal customers and should be involved in design, review and validation efforts for better results. This simple advice is often ignored by project team members.

There are various thoughts on the time frame and the interviews. It can be in one go, periodic or may be spread out over the life cycle of the project. Thus a series of interviews can be conducted at the start and the summary of these initial conversations can be given back to interviewers for review and early model revisions can be shared with the job holders. Thus the total amount of investigation time may be less than that used upfront with focus groups.

Whatever may be the approach, the question is 'how much is enough?' There is no absolute or correct number of interviews that guarantees completeness in a soft information situation; a good behavioural guideline is 'closure'. The check is when the same topics keep coming up and significant new information is no longer being generated. Closure for a relatively stable job might occur after merely one or two interviews, in contrast to a multi-location case for worker position, where a closure may not be achieved even after ten or more interviews.

Behavioural Event Interview

Behavioural Event Interview (BEI) is an interview technique based on the premise that the best predictor of future behaviour is past behaviour. BEI allows the interviewer to:

- Gain detailed job-related examples
- Assess past performance
- Assess competencies

The aim is to improve the fit between the candidate and the position (see Fig 5.1).

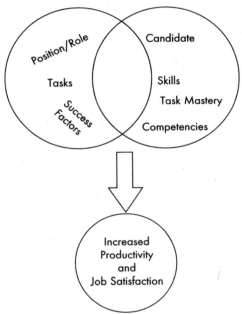

The overriding objective is to improve the
fit between the candidate and the position.

Fig. 5.1: Aims of BEI

The purpose of BEI, as shown in Fig. 5.2, is to best match the candidates' skills, competencies and motives with the requirements and success factors of the position.

It is widely recognized that selection interviews are prone to problems such as bias and show inadequacy as predictors of performance. However, they are also the most popular selection method and serve a number of important functions, such as providing the interviewee with an opportunity to ask questions about the job and the organization.

What is the purpose of using BEI?

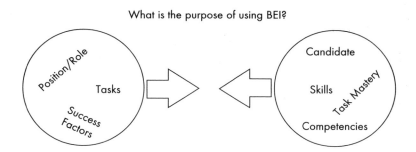

Fig. 5.2: Purpose of BEI

Fortunately, there are techniques that help improve the effectiveness of interviews. Often referred to under the name of 'structured interviews', these techniques represent a variety of ways to improve fairness and accuracy in predicting performance. In fact, the degree to which the interview is structured is less important than the core principle of focusing on job-related criteria. Questions asked usually facilitate the gathering of information relevant to key job requirements. Judgements are formed by evaluating this evidence against criteria that have been established through analysing the job or role—rather than by directly comparing candidates on the basis of the interviewer/s overall impressions.

Behavioural Description Interview (BDI)

BDI is a version of BEI, one of the main competency definition techniques. Both are related to the Critical Incident Technique (CIT), but differ from it in the scope and length of the examples or 'events' that interviewees are asked to describe and in the trigger questions that are used by the interviewer to elicit these examples. The BDI and BEI techniques are considered to be more suitable for complex jobs (such as management roles) or those involving a high level of interpersonal skill (such as sales roles). This is because they elicit a small number of examples of complex behaviour, which can then be explored in depth, whereas a Critical Incident interview may elicit up to a hundred brief examples. We have found BDI to be highly effective, even at the most senior levels, including that of a chief executive.

The BDI and BEI are also not restricted to 'critical' aspects of the job, but can be adapted to explore any key requirement. This is done by designing specific eliciting questions—in the case of BDI these questions are developed to gather information on particular competencies (criteria) which have been identified as important for the role in question. While the eliciting questions are likely to be standardized for all interviewees in a particular assessment context, the rest of the interview does not follow a predetermined structure. Instead, open-ended questions are used to draw out a detailed description of what the candidate did, said, thought and felt during the event he or she has chosen to talk about. The interviewer keeps detailed notes, which are later studied and evaluated against the relevant competencies (criteria) as given in Table 5.1.

Behavioural Event Interviewing Methodology

Step One—Open the Interview

Use the opening to build rapport, make the candidate feel at ease and explain the purpose and expectations of the interview. Here is a suggested opening: Greet the candidate. Introduce the candidate to the panel, including his or her name, position and function within the government/organization. Make the candidate feel at ease. Make small talk.

Explain the purpose of the interview: The purpose of the interview today is to determine whether there is a match between his/her interests and qualifications and the position that is to be filled.

To enable the government/organization to make a proper decision, ask the candidate to spend a few minutes talking about his/her previous work and work-related experience and career history.

Then ask about some events or situations where he/she played a key role. Ask the candidate to focus on situations that occurred within the past 12 to 24 months and which are most relevant to the individual's work. It is much easier to recall recent events than events that occurred in the distant past. Then, at the end of the interview, ask the candidate if there is anything he/she might want to know about the job or position.

If at any time the candidate does not understand a question, ask him/her to let the panel know. Inform the candidate that it would take approximately one and a half hours to conduct the interview.

Mention interruptions and note-taking during the interview. As the organization is looking for a certain type of information, it may be necessary for the panel to interrupt the candidate for more details. Although the former should be interested in whatever the candidate has to say, we should keep it as focused as possible, to get the maximum amount of information in the time available. Notes should be taken during the interview in order to be able to remember all the information the candidate shares.

Once the questions have been asked, give the candidate an opportunity to ask some of his/her own questions or add additional information that he/she considers important for you to know.

Ask if there are any questions before getting started.

Remember you are here to make a decision, so be sure to get as much information as you can on paper in order to make an accurate assessment of the candidate. As you will have to compare competency ratings with your colleagues, remember to record specific behavioural events that the candidate mentions. You are looking for evidence of what the candidate actually did, how he/she did it and what was the nature of the thinking process. Take notes on evidence that relates to these types of events.

Step Two—Review the Candidate's Career History

Work-related Experience and Career Overview
Review the candidate's career development and key job responsibilities. As you hear evidence of technical skills, probe for more information about the candidate's technical knowledge and

expertise. Here is an introductory statement and some follow-up questions:

> I would like you to discuss briefly your career history. Let's start with your most recent position. Why don't you give me a sense of the major things you've done and were accountable for.

What was his/her position? What were the responsibilities? Did he/she have any direct reports? How many? What key skills were required in the job? What technical abilities did the candidate possess which he/she feels are relevant to this job? How have those skills been demonstrated? Which of the previously held positions does the candidate feel best prepares him/her for this job?

(Using the following pages as reference, probe for more details about the candidate's technical knowledge and skills that relate to the job.)

Step Three—Conduct-focused Behavioural Event Interview

Focused Behavioural Event Interview

It is at this time in the interview when you get into detailed behavioural probing with the candidate. Here is a suggested outline for explaining the process to the candidate:

Ask for specific details to be able to see the candidate 'in action'; what they did, said, thought and felt (e.g., get enough detail as if you were going to write a screenplay or shoot a movie).

Ask the candidate to focus on work-related experiences within the last 12 to 24 months. Instruct him/her to use the word 'I' instead of 'we' and be specific rather than general, for example, instead of saying, 'I raised the issue', he/she would be expected to say, 'I said to my colleague, I think you have to consider all the facts.' Explain that you will interrupt the candidate to get more details. Ask the candidate, 'Do you have any questions before we get started?' Tell the candidate, 'Your work experience gives me a better sense of your background. Now I would like to move on and talk about specific job-related situations that you've encountered during the recent past.'

Tell the candidate what type of situation you would like him or her to talk about. Ask for a brief overview, followed by what led up to the situation. Ask for three to five key actions in the situation and the outcome.

Once the candidate has given you an overview of a situation pertaining to a competency question, introduce the detailed probing that would follow. You might say, 'I would like you to go back to the beginning and walk me through the experience—the key elements of the experience as far as your involvement is concerned—in detail. Remember our goal is to have enough material to write a "screenplay" about you, so focus on your role and your perspective.'

- **Customer Interviews**—Contact mapping is about knowing the inside out of customers' needs whereas interviews find out the customers' needs, projecting required competencies. Customer interviews in the context of competency are asking about needs not performance. The goal is customer services rather than how we are doing. The caller should be qualified to discuss the products and customers and on the basis of responses, recognize competency-related information when it comes up. The questions may be structured around the following issues:
  - o What makes your job title the best?
  - o What makes your job title the worst?
  - o What competencies does it require to be good?
  - o What competencies rate it as the worst?
  - o What competencies should the people improve upon?
  - o What are the threats and challenges in your business?
  - o What are the strengths and weaknesses?
  - o How well are you meeting your needs?
  - o What are the other companies doing to meet the needs?
  - o What are the best practices?
  - o What can be done to better meet your needs?

These questions are prime sources of competency information and are critical to help an organization meet its desired business outcomes.

- **Supplier Interviews**—Similar to customers, suppliers provide a push-through approach. They have a broader perspective of the market and the industry as they deal with a wide range of competitors. Getting candid feedback from a supplier is a bit more complicated since the supplier does not want to irritate its customer—the organization. However, the questions may be structured in the following manner:

o Why is your best customer satisfied with the product?
o Why is your worst customer dissatisfied with the product?
o What competencies do the people need to have?
o What should the organization do to get our people to perform the best?

This is a rather straightforward approach in a competency modelling effort.

- **Employee Interviews**—The employees' interview is a very important source of information. A group of employees with a good performance record can be asked:

  o What knowledge and skills are required for the job?
  o What are the attributes of your success?
  o What makes you good at obtaining business results?
  o What are the competencies one should possess in your position?
  o How would these help others to become more effective in their position?
  o How can others become more effective?

Another group of less successful employees may be asked the following questions:

- How skilled were you when you started with the job?
- What would you tell someone who is just a beginner?
- Now knowing the requirement, how could you have better prepared yourself for the job?
- What are the competencies needed for that job position?
- What can you do now to become more effective?

The responses to such questions can be analysed to identify competencies.

- **Supervisor Interviews**—Supervisors have the best perspective concerning competencies required for a position. They would have worked on those positions, dealt with customers or been involved in the hiring process and are the final link between the management and the frontline. They can be asked:

  o Who are the best employees and why are they so effective?
  o Who are the worst employees and why are they so ineffective?
  o What competencies are required to succeed in the particular job position?
  o What are the major problems they come across when dealing with seniors?
  o What is the major encouragement that they received when dealing with seniors?

Supervisors can provide the most candid interview of any group. They focus on the practical competency issues that improve business results. Such interviews can also provide early warnings of potential problems either in the overall process or in the specifics of a competency model.

Teams

Focus groups or work teams is a structured method of gathering competency information. Herein, organizations are required to assemble a team of employees at a single location for days, to provide the group with a trained facilitator familiar with operations of the teams and competency modelling. They should also possess cross-functional skills. An HR professional with job analysis experiences, a trainer for related courses, a supplier, a customer and an industry or HR consultant may form a project team. Stakeholders from different positions may form a group; however, including at least one member employee who is not a stakeholder is helpful. Ideally, the team should consist of five to seven individuals plus a facilitator. The focus group is directed to provide information on the following:

- Job list
- List of accountability and responsibility

- List of major projects or contracts
- Decisions
- Internal and external customer contacts
- Competencies with description
- Measures of evaluation

Initially, the group is to develop a complete list of tasks for the position under analysis. The group can use documented sources and all other possible sources, responsibilities, active projects, customer contacts and decisions with the ultimate goal to capture knowledge, skills and behaviour aspects required for the positions.

It will be useful to discuss the measurements of tasks identified. This will be the basis of building an assessment instrument for the position.

Benchmarking

Whether interviews or feedback, the important parameter in the development of the models is creating a benchmark of those employees who exceed and fall below performance standards. The units between actual business results and competencies provide a radically different view of the model. This indicates the anecdotal nature of soft information approaches and the importance of using a variety of input sources and viewpoints.

In the late 1970s and early 1980s the magazine *Purchasing* published the results of an annual contest in which readers were invited to nominate outstanding sales representatives. Respondents were asked to identify the top three characteristics of these representatives and the winner and their customers were later interviewed. The authors performed a content analysis of the surveys from 1977 through 1983 and tabulated the frequencies for traits that were mentioned by buyers. The long-term averages are shown in Table 5.1. Note that trait numbers 2, 4, 7 and 10 refer to category-level general competency issues. Note also that the only trait related to the sales call that made the *Purchasing* list were numbers 8 and 9. This may be related to one of the most important sources mentioned earlier: customer feedback. This research is nearly 20 years old and has been validated repeatedly by later research and is still being ignored by many sales organizations.

Table 5.1: Sales Competencies Deserved by Customers

Sales Traits		Average Per cent Mentions
1.	Thoroughness and follow through	65
2.	Knowledge of his/her product line	59
3.	Willingness to go to bat for the buyer with the supplier's firm	54
4.	Market knowledge and willingness to keep the buyer posted	41
5.	Imagination in applying his/her products to the buyer's needs	23
6.	Knowledge of buyer's product lines	18
7.	Diplomacy in dealing with operating departments	16
8.	Preparation for well-planned sales calls	12
9.	Regularity of sales calls	9
10.	Technical education	7

Using this as a benchmark, researcher Larry Craft further analyzed the most successful salespeople at a major life insurance company. Using a personality profile questionnaire, insurance professionals identified as top performers scored high in:

- Emotional Intensity: The salesperson's sense of urgency or drive towards short-term goals.
- Intuition: The degree to which a person relies upon experiences and feelings to make a decision, as opposed to complex analysis of the subject matter.
- Assertiveness: An individual's ability to control the actions of others.

Top performers were characterized as 'high ego drive' individuals. Craft recommended that organizations train these trailblazer individuals and provide them with ready support for their questions and problems.

A related benchmarking study similarly used expert-modelling techniques to analyze superior insurance salespeople. Expert modelling requires documenting (writing, audiotape or videotape) everything the salesperson does. Notes are made during and directly after sales calls. A five-year study of top producers found that:

- Top salespeople almost never follow a canned, step-by-step sales call.
- Top salespeople are more customer oriented than product oriented.
- Top salespeople vary their speech to mimic customers' patterns.
- Top salespeople use stories and metaphors to make their point.
- Top salespeople learn how prospects make buying decisions, in order to understand how to sell to them.
- Top salespeople are flexible enough to change a prescribed selling approach if the customer is ready to buy.

These models are not only different from what customers and managers identified, they are radically different from each other too. This shows the anecdotal nature of soft information approaches—even relatively structured ones such as expert modelling. It illustrates the importance of using a variety of input sources and viewpoints. Internal views tend to focus on selling activities and external views concentrate on service factors. Both should be taken into account when developing a competency model.

Established Models

Other than starting from scratch and developing a model, another resource is to adapt a completed model from an outside source as given in Chapter 2. For an organization going through a transition phase, the available documented process or collection of data on past work is of less value. In this situation a model available may be adopted and changes may be brought into focused, towards continuous development.

Management Directed

The model may be dictated by the top management. If strategic decisions are taken to expand the market, add products or change technology, the necessary competencies will be required. In some cases, specially for new ventures, the data does not exist; systems and procedures are not in place, and no industry-specific model is available. Management should give directions explaining the strategy—what the organization needs to do. This is the way to move forward in the process of model development.

Third-party Models

Are there any available competency models that organizations could start with? A number of organizations have developed competency models. The various models give way to many ideas for proceeding, but the existence of many options also makes it difficult to select the best.

Many organizations prefer to develop custom models with significant standardization of processes. A generic competency model is common to all positions that comprise two-thirds of the employees. The rest of the competencies may be competencies specific to various positions.

While developing models, the project team after reviewing all the potential sources have to select their research approach by design rather than by default. The research base must support the accuracy and validity of the model and its assessment process. Each competency is defined, and has a common vocabulary and purpose. A competency model thus comprises of the position of a model; consisting of competencies, definitions and standards by positions and assessment. The summarized format of sources of Competency Information is given below in Table 5.2.

Table 5.2: Sources of Competency Information

Job Title _____

Other Details _____

CATEGORIES

By Assumption _____

(*contd.*)

Table 5.2 (*contd.*)

By Law

By Industry

By Organization

By Work Group

By Background Information

POSITION DOCUMENTATION

Industry Research

Vendor Information

Customer Feedback

Regulations

Certification Requirements

Quality Programmes

PROCESS DOCUMENTATION

Procedure Manuals and Flowcharts

(*contd.*)

Table 5.2 (*contd.*)

Value-added Flowcharts

Time Log Job Task Analysis

Customer Contact Maps

EXISTING DOCUMENTS

Job Description

Union Contracts

Development Planning Documents

Performance Plans

Appraisal Forms

PERSONNEL DEVELOPMENT RESOURCES

Training

INTERVIEWING

Customers

Suppliers

(*contd.*)

Table 5.2 (*contd.*)

Employees

_____

Supervisors

_____

_____

TEAMS

Focus Group/Cross-functional Teams

_____

_____

BENCHMARKING

Superstars

_____

Expert Modelling

_____

_____

ESTABLISHED COMPETENCY MODELS

Management Directed

_____

Third-party Models

_____

For the formation of a competency framework a combination of abilities, aptitudes, skills, qualities, personality traits, interests, motivations, styles and competencies can be assessed by different techniques or a combination of techniques.

Using the above-mentioned techniques and from one's own experience, one can draw a job profile particularly for one's own job. It is basically a list of characteristics, traits and skills that are required to do a particular job well. It also includes the list of 'jobs' one has to do in a particular position. For example, a manager is a decision-maker and thus to take decisions he/she should also show commercial awareness, tolerate ambiguity, etc., and should also have the ability to do these jobs well. Competency mapping is concerned with the second part. It measures whether a person has the competencies to do a particular task well.

Case in Point—One

Various organizations will have information in different forms spread over organization chart, procedures, roles and responsibilities. In a manufacturing industry, the source of information was the Organization chart—Functional Heads (Template 1); Sequence of Operation for Production of XYZ (Template 2); Quality Management Systems—General Requirements, Documentation Requirements (Templates 3, 4); Quality Management System—Quality Manual (Template 5); Control of Documents (Template 6); Control of Records (Template 7); Management Responsibility—Management Commitment, Customer Focus, Quality Objectives, Responsibility and Authority (Template 8, 9, 10, 11); Measurement, Analysis and Improvement—Monitoring and Measurement (Template 12) and Performance Appraisal (Template 13). Such information, which is available with the organization needs to be analyzed thoroughly for better understanding of critical success factors. This is followed by BEI and other interviews for developing the Framework of Competency.

Template 1

XYZ Co. Ltd.—Organization Chart—Functional Heads

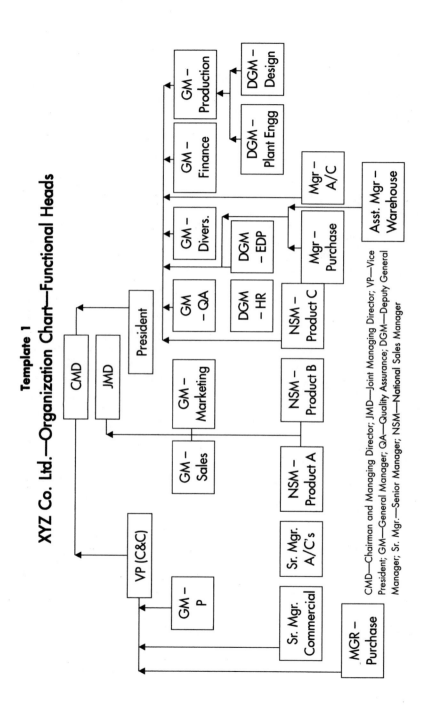

CMD—Chairman and Managing Director; JMD—Joint Managing Director; VP—Vice President; GM—General Manager; QA—Quality Assurance; DGM—Deputy General Manager; Sr. Mgr.—Senior Manager; NSM—National Sales Manager

Template 2

Sequence of Operation for Production of XYZ

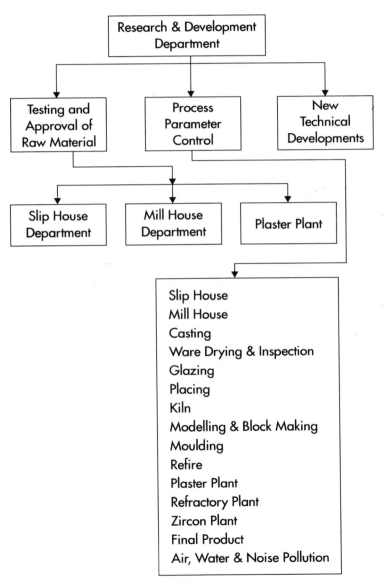

Research & Development Department

Testing and Approval of Raw Material

Process Parameter Control

New Technical Developments

Slip House Department

Mill House Department

Plaster Plant

Slip House
Mill House
Casting
Ware Drying & Inspection
Glazing
Placing
Kiln
Modelling & Block Making
Moulding
Refire
Plaster Plant
Refractory Plant
Zircon Plant
Final Product
Air, Water & Noise Pollution

Template 3
ISO – 9001: 2000

Quality Management System

General Requirements

We have established, documented, implemented and maintained a quality management system to continually improve it's effectiveness in accordance with this international standard by implementing the following:

- Identification of the process.
- Determining the sequence and interaction of these processes.
- Determining criteria and methods for effective operational control.
- Information availability to support operational monitoring—measurement, monitoring and analysis of processes.
- Planning actions for continuous improvement.

Template 4
ISO – 9001: 2000

Quality Management System

Documentation Requirements

Our quality management system is documented, which includes:

- Quality policy and quality objectives.
- Quality manual.
- Documented procedures required by this international standard.
- Documentation needed by an organization to ensure effective planning, operation and control of it's processes.
- Records required by this international standard.

Template 5
ISO – 9001: 2000

Quality Management System

Quality Manual

The quality management system manual includes:

- Quality manual (level 1).
- Departmental manual covering all mandatory procedures (level 2).
- Work instructions which describe how a specific activity is to be performed at all department levels (level 3).
- Records and applicable external documents related to standards and customers (level 4).

Template 6
ISO – 9001: 2000

Quality Management System

Control of Documents

A management representative is responsible for maintaining all controlled documents related to ISO 9001: 2000 requirements. Control of documents includes the following steps:

- All the departmental heads have a master list of the documents pertaining to their areas.
- All documents are given an identification number for easy reference.
- Whenever a revised document is received/issued, document control procedure is followed.
- Management representative maintains a list which indicates the latest revision status of the document for the entire organization.
- Obsolete documents are returned to the management representative; only one copy is kept, stamped 'OBSOLETE' for reference and all the other copies are destroyed.

- Prior to issue, documents are approved by the person who is authorized to do so.
- It is ensured that the latest issues of the documents are available when they are needed.
- Changes to the documents are approved by people who have background information so that they can make the right decision when checking the changes.
- Control documents are stamped 'CONTROLLED COPY' in ink that is of any colour other than black.
- Documents of external origin are identified and controlled.

Template 7
ISO – 9001: 2000

Quality Management System

Control of Records

Records are maintained to demonstrate:

- Compliance with quality management system
- Performance related to achieving objectives and targets

The records include operational records, training records, internal/external audits and management review records.

The records are legible, readily identifiable to the relevant operational activity. They are protected against damage or loss.

Unless specified otherwise, records are retained for one year.

Template 8
ISO – 9001: 2000

Management Responsibility

Management Commitment

Our organization is committed to the development and implementation of the quality management system and continual improvement by ensuring the following:

- Customer requirement is explained to all employees in order to satisfy the customer.
- The statutory and regulatory requirements related to the product are explained to all employees. These include external standards, weights and measure act, packaging act.
- Quality policy is understood and implemented by all employees.
- Quality objectives and targets are established at the company as well as all departmental levels.
- Adequate resources are made available.
- Management review of the quality management system is carried out at necessary intervals.

Template 9
ISO – 9001: 2000

Management Responsibility

Customer Focus

We have documented the following:

- The external/internal customer requirements at all department/ operational manual level.
- To determine the specific requirements of a customer, including requirements for delivery and post-delivery activities.
- Latent need of customer for specified or intended use.

Template 10
ISO – 9001: 2000

Management Responsibility

Quality Objectives

Procedure for Measurement of Objectives

1. Overall production efficiency is calculated in terms of percentage on the basis of number of finished products sent to the warehouse vs. total moulds filled in the casting department.

% of efficiency

$$= \frac{\text{Total number of finished products sent to the warehouse}}{\text{Total moulds filled in the casting department}} \times 100$$

2. Customer satisfaction is measured on the basis of the customer complaints received from the market.

% of customer complaint

$$= \frac{\text{Total number of complains received}}{\text{Total number of pieces dispatched in the domestic market}} \times 100$$

3. The pitcher ware is measured in terms of percentage

$$\% \text{ of pitcher} = \frac{\text{Total number of pitcher wares}}{\text{Total number of once-fired pieces sorted}} \times 100$$

Template 11
ISO – 9001: 2000

Management Responsibility

Responsibility and Authority

1. Chairman and Managing Director

The Chairman and Managing Director of the company has control over all the affairs of the company. In his capacity as Chairman and Managing Director, he presides over the meeting of the company's Board of Directors. It is his responsibility to ensure proper planning and execution of the policy and programme, as laid down by the Board of Directors for the growth and prosperity of the company, as well as to look after the interest of the shareholders of the company.

2. Joint Managing Director

The Joint Managing Director facilitates the above listed programmes and policies of the company.

3. Vice President

The Vice President is responsible for general administration and production co-ordination including manpower planning, public relations, smooth administration, planning and execution of work relating to economical activities in new projects. He is authorized to sign cheques jointly with another bank signatory and also to sign a Purchase Order in accordance with the mandatory limits set from time to time.

Template 12
ISO – 9001: 2000

Measurement, Analysis and Improvement

Monitoring and Measurement

An organization has a determined and established process for the measurement of quality management performance. Customer satisfaction is used as a measure of system output and internal audit is used as a tool for evaluating ongoing system compliance.

- An organization monitors information and data on customer satisfaction and dissatisfaction. The methods and measures for obtaining customer satisfaction information, data, and the nature and frequency of reviews is defined.

We have established a process for performing objective audits in order to determine if the quality management system has been effectively implemented and maintained. It conforms that an audit programme is planned taking into consideration the status and importance of the processes, to identify potential opportunities for improvement.

- Audit process, including the schedule, is based on the status and importance of activities, areas or items to be audited and the results of the previous audit.
- The procedure for internal audit covers the audit scope, frequency and methodologies, as well as the responsibilities, requirements for conducting audits, as well as recording and reporting results to the management.
- Audits are performed by personnel other than those who perform the audit.

Template 13

Performance Appraisal

A.1 Performance Measurement System—Employees on the job, performance is to be measured on the basis of the target fixed and cumulative results achieved in the year 200_ –200_

Key Results Areas	Achievement Last Year	Target Current Year	Achievement				Cumulative	
			Q1	Q2	Q3	Q4	Target	Achievement
1.								
2.								
3.								
4.								
5.								
6.								

Suggestions

Q-1
1.
2.
3.
4.

Q-2
1.
2.
3.
4.

Q-3
1.
2.
3.
4.

Q-4
1.
2.
3.
4.

Signature of the Appraisee:

Signature of the Appraiser:

Signature of the Reviewer:

Case in Point—Two

In a telecommunication organization the unique role/s were identified for which the job/position competency model is to be developed. The information gathered for developing the model is primary responsibility, reporting structure, key results areas, people responsibilities, financial authority and primary interaction; internal and external.

Unique Role

Unique Role Code	Geo-Postpaid
Unique Role Name	Postpaid Zonal Lead
Line of Business	Wireless Postpaid
Function	Sales
Number of incumbents in this unique role	As per the Zone Structure of the circle

Primary Responsibility

The role is responsible for:

1. The customer integrated operations have two critical functions—customer service delivery and subscriber acquisition through the World Web Express (WWE) architecture.
2. Channel partner: Number—Capillarity, Productivity
3. Customer Integrated Operational Units (CIOU) Collections

The role has to provide guidance and direction for the WWEs for enhancing postpaid business as well as participating in the prepaid acquisition and recharge sales.

The Role has to work closely with the Cluster Head to achieve business goals as follows:

- Achievement of Postpaid & Prepaid Sales Targets ____ Nos.
- Achievement of Collection Target Rs. ____ Mn.

- Local marketing activities: Signages, Merchandizing and Promotions.
- Coordinate with Care, B and C teams.
- Relationship management with the assigned customer-base of the CIOU.

  o Physical and telephonic contact with the customer-base and committed problem resolution through organization.
  o Designing of special offers for the assigned customer-base in order to ensure up-selling, cross-selling and references.

- Ensuring adequate capillarity of Convergence Plus (CPs) and Fiber Optic Services (FOS) to meet prospecting norms and conversion rates, that in turn lead to target achievement.

  o Outbound Sales FOS = minimum 3/WWE
  o Collection FOS = 1 FOS/500 Customers

- FOS callage and productivity enhancement through daily monitoring.

  o Daily calls per FOS = 15/day
  o Daily calls by Zonal Lead = 5/day

- Tracking Web World Express (WWE) Return on Investment (ROI) on an ongoing basis and initiating corrective measures for enhancing WWE returns. Helping the WWE franchisee to attain store viability in as short a time as possible.

  o Weekly review meetings with the Zonal Team and WWE team for business development.
  o Structured lead generation activities to increase the size of the prospect funnel.
  o Initiating action for churning high Average Revenue per User (ARPU) competition customers.
  o Maximizing collections from the customer base to 95 per cent + levels.
  o Timely and proactive market intelligence feedback to cluster head WWE:

    ◆ Proper manning and deployment of trained staff.
    ◆ Deployment of all processes/systems for acquisitions/ fulfilment.

- ◆ Stock availability with CPs/WWEs.
- ◆ Promotions: upsell—cross-sell

Reporting Structure

Reports To	Unique Role	Role Code
Functionally	Cluster Head	Geo-Sales — GS01
	Or Cluster Postpaid Lead (if appointed)	Geo-Sales — GS02
Administratively		

Roles Reporting into this Role	Unique Role	Role Code	No. of Incumbents
From within organization			
From related companies	Promoters.		
	Agency — roll staff		
From outside	FOS & Sales Telecallers		

Key Results Areas (KRAs)

(KRA 70%, RR 20%, ICA 10%)

Perspective	KRA-Measures	Weightage	Target	Actual	Rating
Financial	Sales Targets – Postpaid	40%			
	Sales Targets – Prepaid (Through POS, WWE, Key retail A/c)	20%			
	Channel Capillarity: _____ POS _____ WWE _____ new CP appointment	10%			
	Channel Productivity: _____ POS _____ WWE _____ new CPs	10%			
	WWE profitability and ROI	10%			
Customer	Retention of top 10 per cent Customers (ARPU) & Churn <1 per cent in this category	10%			
	Routine Responsibilities	*Weightage*			
	Channel Partner and WWE coverage: Callage _____ /week	30%			
	Brand Visibility within the territory, Plan and product awareness though promotions	25%			

(contd.)

(contd.)

	Weightage
Training of staff at WWE and Channel partners — Training hours	15%
Customer Relation management—issue resolution, special offers	15%
Competition Tracking—products, tariffs, key outlets	15%
Individual Contribution Areas	
Special Projects e.g. Market reach of open Mkt H/s	50%
Acquisition from cross-selling to customer base	50%

People Responsibilities

Area	Responsibility
Recruitment	WWE Franchisees, Channel Partners and FOS
Training	Class Room Training on Products, Tariff's, Processes and competition offers/practices to all customer facing units. Selling, Negotiation and Objection Handling Skills to FOS. Demonstrating sales techniques on the job—leading by example.
Career Development	Coaching and career development of Team Leader and key FSD/FOS for enhancing productivity
Performance Appraisal	Structured Review of all CIOU's and FSD/FOS
Job Allocation	
Administrative (Leave sanction etc.)	Yes (FOS)

Financial Authority

Area	Authority
Revenues	Meeting monthly collection and sales targets.
Profit	
Collections	Achieve 95 per cent + collection and reduce outstanding collections. Regular review of CIOU collection performance along with the collection team.
Budget	Imprest for local promotional activities, subject to approval of the Circle Postpaid Head.
Expense Approval	Ratifying all WWE claims prior to submission.
Negotiation	Ensuring customer satisfaction through addressing pending issues and convincing trade and customers on objections, if any.
Cost Reductions	

Primary Interactions—Internal

Who	Why (Purpose)
Cluster Head or Cluster Postpaid Lead	Clarity on day to day objectives /operational issues requiring support. Prioritize tasks and resource deployment. Overall strategy dissemination and review. Target vs. achievement analysis, road blocks, promotional support, training and other input planning.
Cluster Customer Care Team	Regular interaction with Zonal CC to drive SLAs at WWE. Work towards 100 per cent FTR at WWE's and ensuring loop closure for all cases.
Cluster Commercial Team	Regular interaction with Commercial leads to ensure system adherence and process compliance, claim settlement on time, collection data feedback, follow-up on ensuring daily remittance of collections and other amounts, etc.

Primary Interactions—External

Who	Why (Purpose)
FOS of Channel/ Channel Partners	Daily Performance Review of WWE and FOS, target setting, tactical activity planning, market feedback, process/tariff communication, prospecting and lead generation activities, collection review, etc.
Consumers	Customer contact for relationship building, issue handling and lead generation.
Promoters	Smooth and effective execution of lead generation activities and product promotion.
Channel mapped to CIOUs	Relationship building and business enhancement.

CHAPTER SIX

Competency Mapping and Assessment Centres

IDENTIFICATION of competencies and the development of competency models, both generic and specific, is finally achieved after going through a rigorous process. Linked with the HR systems, the competency model is applied in the various HR functions. Chapter Four exhibits various formats to map the various competencies with the HR functions. These assessments are based on observation, facts, probing questions, BEIs, other interviews, behaviours perceived, performance and results achieved. However, there is also a need to assess these competencies by other techniques in order to validate the assessment of the panelists, peers, superiors and others. Competency is to be mapped on the supply side (Fig. 6.1) (both internal and external supply) with the developed competency framework model to the job requisition. Competencies—namely, knowledge, skills, traits, motives—have to be integrated with the HR system. An assessment centre is an alternative to validate the

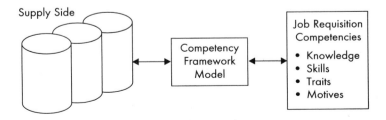

Fig. 6.1: Competency Mapping Model

competencies with the help of various tools. This is the most important step in mapping the competencies once they have been identified.

How were the People Assessed Earlier

The assessment centre is a method or an approach that is used to make decisions about people—to choose them, promote them or to put them on a 'fast-track' scheme. The objective is to obtain the best possible indication of people's current or potential competence to perform at the target job or job level. The assessment is observed by a team of assessors. It is a combination of methods, which comprises of simulations of the key elements of the job under the headings of various companies, the assessment through all methods/techniques is brought together to indicate what is crucial for high performance.

A History of Assessment Centre

Assessment Centre in the UK

How were the people assessed earlier? This approach of an assessment centre in organizations started just two decades back. Looking into history, in 1942 War Office Selection Boards (WOSB) were introduced in the UK to select officers. Anstey (1989) recounts that the system where the boards replaced had clearly broken down. A high percentage of people who had passed had to be returned to the unit because of their lack of ability. The old system relied on interviewing people who had been judged as likely to be of officer quality. The judgement was formed on the basis of their background or their achievement in the ranks. These achievements could range from gallantry to exceptional smartness. With this method of pre-selection the old system missed even the chance of interviewing many people who actually had bad officer potential, furthermore, it incorrectly ascribed potential to a large number of those it did get to assess.

The new system was decided upon by the Directorate for the Selection of Personnel and included leaderless group exercises, objective selection tests and separate personal interviews by three assessors. The panel of assessors included a senior officer, a junior officer and a psychiatrist. Anstey describes how the new procedure resulted in a 'dramatic rise' in the success and led to its acceptance throughout the Army.

Assessment Centre in the USA

In the USA, the pioneering work undertaken by the Office of Strategic Studies used the method to select spies during the Second World War (MacKinnon 1977). In the USA, post-war development moved to the private sector. The pioneer was the American Telephone and Telegraph Company (AT&T), which used assessment centres in its management progress study, which began in 1956 (Bray 1964) to investigate changes in personal characteristics as managers moved through their careers. This led to the use of Assessment Centre (AC) as an aid in selecting first-line supervisors, higher-level managers and other specialists.

They assessed 422 lower-level managers who were mostly of white-male origin. They were considered to be representative of AT&T's future middle- and upper-level managers. In the 1970s they initiated a new study of 344 lower-level managers, about half of whom were women and about one-third were minorities. They found that women had advantages in administrative ability, interpersonal skills and sensitivity, written communication skills, energy and internal work standards. Men had advantages in company loyalty, motivation to advance in the company, attentiveness to power structures. There were no differences in intellectual ability, leadership ability, oral communication skills or stability of performance. The biggest difference was in men's traditionally masculine interests and women's traditionally feminine interests. Putting together the information they determined that women and men had similar management potential. However, race differences were stronger. The most significant finding of this study was that managerial potential is highly predictable. The method was taken up by Standard Oil of Ohio in 1962, then by IBM, Sears, General Electric and JC Penney (Finkle 1976). Its use has increased since the 1980s.

There were differences between the US and UK approaches, which largely stemmed from the original background to their introduction. In the UK a greater emphasis was placed on group exercises with an appointed leader, group discussions and long written exercises, whereas in the US more emphasis was placed on in-tray exercises, leaderless group exercises with assigned roles and two person role plays.

The Use of Assessment Centres in the Industry

Modern assessment centres in the UK tend now to follow the American format although there are still some which have their roots in the public sector civil service model. The growth in the use of assessment centres in the UK has been rapid. In 1986 Robertson and Makin reported that slightly more than one quarter of the organizations who employed 500 people or more used assessment centres. In 1989 Mabey, reported that more than one-third of the companies employing over 1,000 people used them, while most recently Boyle et al. (1995) reported that 45 per cent of the organizations who responded used assessment centres and that their use was more prevalent in the private sector and by larger organizations. The main reason behind this has been the realization that centres have the element of decision making in selection and promotion that can have a demoralizing effect on those individuals who have not been performing. Organizations have also come to realize that to be competitive they must constantly invest in the development of their staff, in order to enable them to respond effectively to an increasingly uncertain market. This has meant that rather than selecting new employees, organizations are now investing more in their existing workforce. Traditionally, companies who wished to train their staff would send them on a training course outside the organization, and there has been an increasing emphasis placed on delivering training that is relevant to the organization's needs and business objectives.

In the UK, a survey by the Industrial Society (1996), based upon 414 replies, found that 59 per cent were using assessment centres for a broad range of staff and 43 per cent were using development centres. A survey by Roffey Park Management Institute (1999) reported broadly similar results. Assessment centres were used by 62 per cent of respondents and development centres were used by 43 per cent. A majority of respondents (57 per cent) also expected the use of both types of centres to increase. The Roffey Park respondents also foresaw a continued move from assessment to development centres. In the USA, Lowry (1996) conducted a survey of public-sector organizations and found that 62 per cent used assessment centers, while 19 per cent used development centres.

The Roffey Park results repeated those of earlier years by showing that both assessment centres and development centres were the province of larger organizations. It was found that assessment centres were used by 29 per cent of the organizations employing up to 50 people, compared with the 72 per cent of the organizations employing more than 5,000 staff.

The centre should be a part of the HR strategy which in turn needs to be linked to the business strategy. The HR strategy aims to ensure that the organization has competent people. Not only does this have to be seen as a vital part by those with power in the organization, it also begs the question: 'Competent' at what cost? Job analysis reveals the typical and representative situations faced by people in the job and what are the main outputs in these situations. The competence model revealed by the job analysis is to be performed effectively in the exercises and tools. If the job analysis competencies are correct and the exercises are well designed as simulations of the job, it will be possible to see the competencies in people's performance of the exercises. If the competencies cannot be observed in the exercises or tools then present exercises need to be revisited for amendment or new ones need to be developed.

To ensure that the competency dimensions are properly covered, it is usual to have a grid of dimensions against the exercises and check off which dimensions will be shown by each exercise. It is important to fine-tune exercises as far as possible to bring out represented dimensions and under-represented dimensions. A grid of competency dimension by exercises is presented in Table 6.1.

All competency dimensions should be measured by at least two assessment tools. If some dimension is more important it should be measured by three or four assessment tools.

Many industry leaders are currently using assessment centres, and their modified forms, to improve their human resources capital. Diverse companies like HUL, Ranbaxy, Tata Group, Tera Nova, HSBC, ICICI, Colgate, Motorola have well-defined assessment centres to look into the overall personal and organizational growth.

An individual's behaviour and effectiveness in a certain job that requires complex behaviour is predicted by multiple KSAs

Table 6.1: Grid of Competency Dimensions by Exercises/Tools

	Interview	Role Play	In Tray	Group Problem	Group Negotiation	Psychometric Test
Breadth of Awareness	*	*		*		*
Clarity of Understanding				*	*	*
Innovative				*		*
Result-oriented			*		*	*
Self-confidence	*		*			*
Sensitivity to Others				*		*
Co-operative		*	*		*	*
Patience	*		*		*	*

(Knowledge, Aptitude, Skills). This leads to the need to identify and then assess KSAs and requires multiple assessment methods and assessors.

Motorola has spent considerable time in developing management competencies based on skills, knowledge and behaviours. Their assessment process involves a series of indoor and outdoor practical team tasks, each with a nominated leader and non-participant observer, whose feedback at the end of the task is also assessed. Rather than being treated as 'tables of stone', these assessment centre scores are used as a basis for discussion from which a short-list of candidates for further interview is agreed upon. The advantage of this process is that if someone with a lower score is short-listed, there are still clear and openly expressed reasons for doing so, thus reinforcing transparency in the whole system.

Tata Steel: As guided by the Tata vision of doubling the revenues every four years, TISCO launched the Performance Ethic Programme (PEP) that focused on the main competencies that are required by their business. The various positions were divided into clusters and jobs, with the top 100 positions requiring the following competencies: Strategy Ability, Entrepreneurship, Efficiency, Communication, Business Understanding, Influencing People Skills and Leadership.

Citibank: Citibank takes a lot of pride in its human capital and focuses on the following values and competencies: Business Opportunity, Leadership, Adaptability, Innovation, Integrity, Relationship and Change Management.

AT&T: This dynamic organization stresses to be amongst the front-runners in the following aspects: Respect, Dedication, High Standard of Integrity, Innovation and Teamwork.

AlliedSignals: AlliedSignals, an advanced technology and manufacturing company, serves customers worldwide with aerospace and automotive products. They identified success attributes, viz., Business Acumen, Customer Focus, Vision and Purpose, Values and Ethics, Bias for Action, Commitment, Teamwork, Innovation, Developing People.

ITC: ITC looks for Strategic Mindset, Customer Focus, Making Things Happen, Leading Change and People Management.

Johnson & Johnson: At Johnson & Johnson, success can be achieved by those who master Complexity, Focus on Organization and People Development, Customer/Market, and Believe in Innovation and Independent partnering.

HUL: The competency model at HUL comprises of Truth and Trust, Courage Competencies of day to day work, Caring for Stakeholders and Customers and being Action-oriented.

Pfizer: Success can be achieved at Pfizer by those who have competencies, viz., Team Work, Leadership, Customer Focus, Innovation and Integrity.

Aventis: Aventis focuses on the competencies: Respect for People, Integrity, Sense of Urgency, Networking, Creativity and Empowerment.

Types of Exercises

- *Written Exercises*—These are simulations of the written work that might be undertaken by the target-level job holder. They are completed by the participants themselves. If the number of such exercises is large they become dull.

- *In-Tray*—The most famous written exercise is the in-tray or in-basket, which simulates the typical pile of papers that might confront a job holder on a particular day. Items are targeted upon particular competencies and it is made clear to participants that it is not a test of delegation. It is important that the participant responds the way in which he/she would in a real-life situation. Nowadays the in-tray might be computed and partly presented to people by computer. The in-tray can also include simulated e-mails.

- *Analytical Exercises and Interactive Exercises*—This type of written exercise involves engaging the participants in an analytical exercise. An issue is given to all participants. In interactive exercises the participants are required to give a written component of the interaction. They may be asked to write the outcome of a group discussion for itself. It provides concrete evidence of the person's cognitive competencies and removes ambiguity.

- *One-to-one Exercises*—These exercises involve role players who play the role. It is essentially an act of fact finding, decision making or negotiation. The choice of the setting, roles or outputs depends on the job analysis. It adds realism though it may be time consuming.

- *Vignettes*—To avoid role plays video-vignettes can be used. The vignettes present participants with videotaped lead-up to a situation with oral responses. It is a form of situational testing; while preserving fidelity, it ensures that participants are presented with a consistent situation.
- *Group Exercises*—These should replicate the key types of groups with whom people in the job will be involved.
- *Harmonizing the Exercises*—The different exercises once drafted need to have standardized instructions and a format of the outcomes. It should be clear; participants should know exactly what the setting is and what they are meant to do.
- *Integrating the Exercises*—An assessment centre can have much more impact if the exercises are clubbed together in an integrated centre. At times the participant may assume a fictional character—a particular manager. There might be some issues which are common across the exercises. At times two role plays might occur as interruptions to the written exercise that contains material relevant to the role plays. Furthermore, the role plays might provide information that helps the participant to complete the written exercise. Integrating the exercises is a bonus and the centre should not distort the goal. It replicates the situations managers usually encounter. It also helps in avoiding replication of the lengthy background information needed before each exercise. One has to ensure that with linkages, somebody who has done badly in one exercise is able to do well in later exercises.
- *Trial of Exercises*—The exercises once developed should be tried out on a group of people who are at the same level in the organization as the people who will go through the centre. The group should be a mix of people based on their performance. The participants should be encouraged for their views and comments. The focus should be on:

  o Clarity of instructions
  o Time limit
  o Difficulty level

The trial run should be video recorded for the assessors' training. The focus can be on two or three participants with difference in the level of competence, so that assessors can concentrate while practising their observation and recording skills.

The desired changes that are considered beneficial need to be incorporated.

It is necessary to decide upon the marking guides for the assessors' training. All possible responses can of course never be anticipated. It is essential for the assessor to understand the competency dimensions and behavioural indicators so that they can interpret in terms of the dimensions and the actual behaviour of participants. Where possible, a 'behavioural framework' for each exercise should be developed. The behavioural anchors should ascertain both positive and negative behaviours that participants may produce for each competency.

Similarly, with written exercises the dimensions that each part of the exercise is targeting should be indicated. If there is more than one dimension it may also be indicated. It provides a check so that the dimensions are addressed properly, thereby a guide to the linkages and issues in the exercises is developed. The more specific the guidelines, the greater the agreement on marking among assessors.

With each exercise there needs to be a response recording sheet. It should give the positive indicators of the competency dimension and the rating scale. The focus should be to record the evidence of negative and positive indicator for the dimension. However, the formatting of the record sheet would vary from exercise to exercise depending upon the nature of outcome and the dimensions.

To summarize the ratings, a rating grid is required. This grid would be a compilation of all exercises together on a rating scale as shown in Table 6.2.

Off-the-shelf Exercises

Off-the-shelf exercises are also available. Exercises which best match the requirement may be chosen. These are readily available and cheaper than developing one's own exercises. But these exercises are not specifically designed with the organizations' competency dimensions in mind. Thus it is difficult to choose a set of exercises that best address the dimensions. In this case the competency

Table 6.2: A Grid for Ratings

Assessment Centre Grid Name _____

Number _____

	Interview	Role Play	In-Tray	Group Problem	Group Negotiation	Psychometric Test	Ratings				
Breadth of Awareness	*	*		*		*	1	2	3	4	5
Clarity of Understanding				*	*	*	1	2	3	4	5
Innovative				*		*	1	2	3	4	5
Result-oriented	*		*		*	*	1	2	3	4	5
Self-confidence	*		*			*	1	2	3	4	5
Sensitivity to Others				*		*	1	2	3	4	5
Co-operativeness		*	*		*	*	1	2	3	4	5
Patience	*		*		*	*	1	2	3	4	5

dimensions are being fitted to the exercises rather than the other way round. These would not have the language of the organization and the buy-in of line managers. These exercises cannot target the particular job or job-level of a particular organization. As they do not simulate the target job, they cannot be sent to preview how the person would behave in the job, though they may simulate some aspects of managerial jobs that are generic across organizations. While assessing, the marks will be less productive of job performance to the extent that the exercises are not a genuine preview of the job. The tray of group exercises are also irrelevant to the target job but are included, simply because most of the organizations have them.

Off-the-shelf exercises, as they do not require involvement during the development, invite lack of understanding which makes training of assessors difficult. The need of parallel versions is particularly strong if the objective is promotional or quasi-development.

However, the advantage is that there is no development cost and off-the-shelf exercises can be obtained immediately. They are developed on the basis of research and possess in-built psychometric properties. They are statistically analyzed and are reliable as well as valid.

Customized Exercises

Somewhere in between off-the-self and tailor-made exercise are customized exercises. Herein the consultant takes a basic exercise and customizes it to the need of the client organization. They are written with the objective in mind, giving a genuine simulation of work at the job or job level in the organization. The in-tray has items that fit into the organization, to be meaningful to the job. All exercises may not be customized, but it will be cheaper than designing tailor-made exercises. However, adapting exercises to the organization may raise certain legal issues on copyright.

External Centre

Another option is to send people to centres run by a consultancy. The advantage is subcontracting a time-consuming procedure. The element of objectivity and independence would be higher. The disadvantage is that the exercises are not tailor-made, but they are a cost-effective alternative if the number of people to be assessed is less.

Non-exercise Material

Though exercises are at the core of the centre, there is a range of other material that is included for assessment. For assessing certain competencies, exercises may not be sufficient; additional information is needed for making decisions based on the overall competency model.

- *Interviews*—Several competency dimensions can be assessed through interviews, in addition to the information provided by exercises. Situational questions can be asked to probe into particular competency dimensions. It may also be used to ask pressure-related questions experienced in the past. The interview has to be carried out systematically if it is confined to measuring certain identified competencies. Thus the dimensions and possible lines of questioning are specified beforehand. The recording is done on the recording sheet as in the case of exercises. Interviews can also be carried out by experts in the external centre based on desirable experience and qualifications.

Ratings by Self and Others

- *Self-assessment*—Self-assessment gets participants to think about themselves in terms of the competency dimensions. Participants may be assessed before the start of the assessment centre and at its conclusion. However, such assessments cannot be relied upon in all cases as people are selecting themselves for a potential job. This is not promising. There might be cases of significant differences between the assessment of assessors and ratings of self-assessment.
- *Peer Assessment*—Peer assessment can be carried out before the assessment centre. This may be an important basis to assess how participants viewed each other before the exercises, comparing it with their contribution at the group exercises. In addition this is a valuable information for selection and also for validity of peer assessment. Major differences in assessment

by peers and assessors may yield important information about line managers' ratings.

Line managers' ratings are valuable as they help in analyzing the relation between the ratings given by them and those by assessors, participants and peers. Another advantage is ensuring the involvement of line managers.

360-degree Feedback

The 360-degree feedback process provides key inputs by helping participants to gain an insight into their strengths and weaknesses. It also becomes the basis for the participants in deciding to try and approach the exercise situations differently.

When implementing the 360-degree appraisal process the following points should be kept in mind:

1. Identify an employee who would benefit from a 360-degree appraisal, consult his/her boss and possibly any relevant HR specialists, with a need to know.
2. Appoint an administrator to co-ordinate the entire process. Also appoint a facilitator, who should be an individual with great experience of personal development and the requisite counselling skills to help the appraisee with the difficult but important task of action planning. Ideally, one person should perform both these roles.
3. Decide between two styles of implementing the process:

   (a) *Open:* The appraisee administers the early stages of the process, choosing who will complete the questionnaires (with the help of the facilitator) and sending out the questionnaires himself/herself.

   (b) *Anonymous:* The process is carried out anonymously with the administrator/facilitator choosing the respondents and sending out the questionnaires. With this method, the appraisee will not know the identification of the rates (except the boss).

4. Depending upon which style of implementation has been selected, either the appraisee or the administrator/facilitator

should decide who is asked to rate, thinking carefully about the selections. Up to three peers and three subordinates from a cross-section of jobs are required to give a wide coverage of views. One or two customers or internal clients should also be included if possible. Raters who are likely to be fair and dispassionate rather than very close friends or sworn enemies, should be chosen. The boss and appraisee must both complete the questionnaire.

5. Once this has been decided, the questionnaires should be sent out with an envelope for return and a letter of explanation to the rater, giving appropriate guarantees about anonymity and confidentiality. If anonymity is required, these materials should be delivered to the rater in an unmarked envelope.

Best Practice

In order to conform to best practice, users should endeavour to adhere at all times to the following principles:

- Experienced HR professionals should be appointed to administer the entire process and ideally, to be the facilitator in the feedback process.
- All appraisees should have access to an experienced facilitator who has the necessary skills.
- Appraisees should be given accurate and satisfactory answers to all their questions or if necessary, referred to someone who is able to do so.
- All questions or complaints should be handled by a qualified person who is not directly involved in the rating process.
- The degree of confidentiality and anonymity (who will see the questionnaires/reports and how will they be used) should be communicated clearly at the outset and adhered to rigidly.
- Feedback should be conducted in an accurate and sensitive manner.
- The implications of the feedback should be fully understood.
- Full support and respect should be provided to every appraisee, irrespective of their performance level.

- Appraisees should be encouraged to share their reports with anyone who might be able to assist with their development.
- The contents of a feedback report should never be revealed to anyone except the appraisee without his/her full agreement.
- Action plans should be completed and implementation should be led and subsequently monitored by the facilitator.
- The shelf-life of the report should be communicated to all.
- The entire process should be monitored and evaluated to ensure that it continues to be efficient and effective.

Rating Forms—All rating forms whether self, peer, line manager or 360-degree feedback, when being designed should be targeting the same competency dimensions which are to be examined at the centre. These forms should be completed before the centre. The forms should be designed in such a way that there is opportunity to display the indicated dimensions in their work and demonstrate each competency at the centre.

Tests and Inventories

Psychometric tests, personality inventories, attitude measures, ability tests, etc., can be combined with the exercises depending upon the information needed. It must be relevant to one or more of the targeted competencies to choose tests and inventories that are expected to add to information about the competency dimensions. Also, there should be a check to determine whether people's scores on the test or inventory actually relate to performance on the competency dimensions. It is important that the organization chooses a test that is appropriate to the centre and its participants.

Personality inventories should also be related to the competencies, so that it is clear that the information provided is useful. The additional information can be used for the feedback, career counselling and development. It might help employees to introspect and enhance their performance. There are various types of personality inventories like 16 Personality Factors (PF), Occupational Personality Questionnaire (OPQ), which give a straightforward measure and can be statistically related to the competency dimensions. Other tests may give more information like Myer Briggs Type Indicator (MBTI), Fundamental Interpersonal Relation Orientation-Behaviour

(FIRO-B) and schemes' measure of career anchors. An in-depth psychological assessment will yield insight into the person, which is valuable to understanding his/her competencies and to reveal the fundamental ways in which the person will need to grow and develop. It is only by understanding oneself that a fundamental change is possible.

Projective Techniques

Another way of getting in-depth information is through the use of projection techniques like Thematic Apperception Test, Rorschach, Incomplete Sentences and Blank. Targeting its own dimensions (rather than using the readymade originals) will be beneficial for the organization. It is recommended to consider developing projective exercises. However, developing such material and interpreting the results is a job that requires great expertise.

Chapter Seven

Resistance and Recommendations

A competency model can help your company achieve its strategic goals only if others within the company are convinced.

While embarking on the campaign to gain the support of key stakeholders, one is likely to face resistance. One has to gain commitment not only of those who have signed off the decision but also of those whose co-operation and goodwill is vital for the success of the project.

Advocate the Project Effectively

Ask yourself the following questions to evaluate the commitment of the employees:

- What makes you believe that a competency model will be an effective tool for the purpose?
- Can you describe the process of developing a model, resources needed and potential applications of the model?
- How do you suggest the process be designed to ensure its success?
- What are the theoretical underpinnings of the process?
- How would you ensure the real, practical, long-term benefits and results?

These questions if not answered will lead to resistance within the organization. Once people know that the business needs are being addressed directly and will facilitate practical human resource decision making, they are more likely to listen.

Identify the Key Stakeholders and the Expected Levels of Support

Before the plan comes into action, list all stakeholders—individuals and groups—who might benefit and also those who have personal reasons for not wanting the implementation.

Categorize Your Stakeholder

Determine the likely gain or loss each one would have from the model if it was to be implemented. Try to answer how this project will benefit your department and how it will affect you personally. Now categorize the reasons. You may expect a varying degree of support. Real commitment is not only to be in agreement that the competency model is needed but in supporting the initiative and compliance. In a worst case scenario there might be resistance to the implementation of the project; this will be most detrimental to the success of your project. In other situation there would be silent resistance, where you might not be aware of the person's opposition until it has already caused damage.

Stakeholders' Map

List all the stakeholders, along with your colleagues involved in the project. Now categorize them on the basis of commitment, compliance, resistance and those most critical. As a next step, further classify them on the basis of those who will be most influenced over the success or failure of the project. Keep collecting more information on these stakeholders and update the stakeholders' map as and when you have new information.

Reasons for Lack of Commitment

Once the stakeholders have been identified, try to determine the likely reasons for their lack of commitment. The reasons can be the following:

- If the purpose of using a competency model is not made clear.
- If people are not involved in the development of the model.
- If people are concerned that they will be expected to behave differently when dealing with their bosses and others.
- If the managers feel that the use of a competency model will limit their power of choice or will increase the quantum of work when selecting, developing and appraising people.

Identify what will be the concern of a stakeholder and address the resistance accordingly.

- People are suspicious and sceptical about how the competency model will be used. Will it address the business needs; if yes, how? When the model is developed for appraisal and compensation or for the 360-degree appraisal there is more anxiety which gives way to rumours: Whatever the objective, whether organizational intervention, or modestly involving just a few people, effective and frequent communication is most important to eliminate resistance for the success of the project. Communicate through all forms of media, meetings, e-mails, bulletin boards, newsletter, etc., and solicit the input of a large number of people to minimize resistance.
- Ego gratification results when the stakeholders do not participate in the development stages of the project. The issues and needs of the stakeholders must be addressed before they are required to devote time and effort to an initiative. The best way to deal with this is to treat the stakeholders as internal customers. Involve as many stakeholders as possible in clarifying the business need, identifying or validating competencies and designing the project implementation. Acknowledge their ideas and involve them in order to resolve issues and win over people. Once you have been successful in persuading them, they will

be converted into committed individuals. Consultative decision is always the best way to overcome resistance.

- A competency project may be seen as a threat to the status quo and may imply that people should change their behaviour. Convert this threat into an opportunity by clarifying the value of the competency model, which in fact will help employees understand what is expected of them, what they can do to develop their strengths and what elements of their jobs they should focus on in order to succeed. It should be shown as a tool for development and success rather than for primitive measurement. It should be further reinforced that what people are doing is right, as well as what they need to do differently.
- To the people the model may appear like a set of formulas. People doubt their instincts and abilities when interacting with people under pre-established, cut-and-dried criteria which replaces their own judgement and skill, choices and decisions. It should be emphasized that the model will give clues about what to look at. There will be a set of behaviours that should be nurtured and would help in assisting how to determine development experiences which are helpful. It would help in doing the jobs better. Especially in situations where expectations of people are changing, it may be emphasized that a competency model allays a lot of fear and anxiety by articulating and clarifying the expectations of everybody concerned.

Resistance and Recommendations: Why and How?

There are chances of resistance on the following issues:

1. *Purpose of a competency model initiative is not made clear.*
   When the purpose of a competency model initiative is not made clear, hold an informal discussion with individuals or teams to review reasons for development and implementation of the model and to answer any questions. Circulate a memo including rationale and details on how you will proceed. Explicitly state the new behaviour required and why. Hold a series of meetings to review the business needs that will be addressed by the competency model.

2. *Need for introducing a competency model into the current human resource system is not seen.*

When the need for introducing a competency model into the current human resource system is not seen, explain what the model will do to make the current system easier. Also describe what is inadequate about the current system and indicate how the model will make the system more effective.

3. *Individuals are not involved in planning the development of the competency model.*

When the development of the competency model does not involve individuals in planning, invite small groups to be advisers during the planning process. Review action plans with individuals who have concerns about timing and solicit ideas on how to adjust or fine-tune the plan. Key stakeholders should be used to identify potential problems and asked to generate ideas to avoid the problems. The deadlines should be flexible, keeping account of critical internal activities such as product introductions, year-end services and the like.

4. *High cost and reward is inadequate for supporting the effort.*

When the cost is high and reward is inadequate for supporting the effort, speak in the 'language of management' regarding cost-benefit, how cost of turnover can be reduced, how training budget can be better focused and how the recruiting cycle can be shortened while reviewing the actions for developing the model. Ideally, where the cost of external resources might be reduced by getting greater participation of internal resources, one may consider using pilots to show the value of the process on a smaller scale before investing in a large-scale project.

5. *Doubt over organizational resources/follow-through to actually finish the development or implementation.*

When organizational resources to actually finish the development or implementation is doubtful, demonstrate visible support by senior management through meetings, memos, etc., which demonstrate committed resources. Change the reward system to encourage the use of the model by stakeholders, to help identify what is necessary to ensure support later. Provide prototypes on how the end-product will actually be applied to human resource systems.

6. *Implementation of model occurs too quickly/slowly.*

   When the implementation of the model occurs either too quickly or too slowly, be on the lookout for signs that the process is losing momentum and call for high-level supporters to show their commitment. Ensure sufficient resources to get the job done. Plan small steps and quick successes to win over sceptics; keep the process simple. It is important to provide a date of accomplishment in order to show progress. The pace of the implementation should be such that the people are not overwhelmed and are sensitive to the other demands of their jobs.

7. *History of poorly implemented changes to human resource systems/processes.*

   When there is a history of poorly implemented changes to human resource systems, do a postmortem with sceptics on why the last one failed—what will it take to avoid the same problems, speak with people in the organization who have implemented major changes successfully.

8. *Concern about what 'using it' really means.*

   When there are concerns about what 'using it' really means, provide training and guidance on the use and implementation of the model. The related tools should be made easier to use with straightforward, stand-alone instructions. Hotlines should be set up to provide tips on the tools. The tools should be tailored to the needs of functions or business so that there is instant credibility.

   Thus each source of resistance needs to be addressed and appropriate action needs to be recommended.

PART TWO

Part One of the book offers the framework for developing a competency model and issues related to developing the model and mapping competency in an assessment centre.

The objective of Part Two is to provide a Generic Competency Model developed after continuous research that can be used by organizations off-the-shelf or customized to their needs.

This part of the book covers the following topics:

- Generic Competency Dictionary
- Generic Competency Model for Leadership Role in any Organization
- Competency Model for HR
- Leadership Competency Model for Automobile Industry

It also provides practical cases developed as an outcome of the consultancy assignments handled in the last few years.

Case In Point:

- One—Hindustan Sanitaryware Industries Ltd.
- Two—Hindustan Petroleum Chemical Ltd. (HPCL)
- Three—Gujarat Heavy Chemicals Ltd. (GHCL)

The given models and sample reports for individual development will be useful for those corporate firms which are still looking to develop the model.

CHAPTER EIGHT

Generic Competency Dictionary

TABLE 8.1 shows the dictionary of various competencies and the related behaviour indicators. The starters can use this off-the-shelf and further customize it for the organization's various positions while developing their own model.

Generic Competency Dictionary

Adaptability

Maintains effectiveness in varying work environments where circumstances and priorities are changing.

Ambition

Is driven to do well, be effective, achieve, succeed and progress quickly through the organization.

Analytical Reasoning

Analyzes, interprets and evaluates complex information arriving at logical deductions and conclusions.

Appraisal

Evaluates subordinates' performance accurately and fairly, providing effective feedback on a regular basis.

Compliance

Adheres to policies and/or procedures, or seeks approval from the appropriate authority before making changes.

Decisiveness

Exhibits a readiness to make decisions, render judgements, take action or commit oneself.

Delegating

Appropriately designates responsibility and refers problems or activities to others for effective action.

Developing Others

Develops subordinates' competence by planning effective experiences related to current and future jobs, in the light of individual motivations, interests and current work situation.

Empathy

Understands the feelings and attitudes of others and is able to put oneself in others' shoes.

Entrepreneurialism

Recognizes and takes advantage of new and/or expanded business opportunities.

Fact Finding

Uses investigative skills and research to gather information relevant to organizational issues, trends and problems.

Flexibility

Is able to modify approach in order to achieve a goal.

Following Through

Establishes procedures and monitors the progress and results of plans and activities to ensure that goals are achieved.

Independence

Takes actions in which the dominant influence is personal conviction rather than the influence of others' opinions.

Influencing

Uses appropriate interpersonal styles, methods of communication, data and arguments to gain agreement or acceptance of an idea, plan or activity.

Initiative/Creativity

Is proactive, self-starting, seizes opportunities and originates action to achieve goals.

Innovation

Is change-oriented and able to generate and/or recognize creative solutions in varying work-related situations.

Integrity

Maintains and promotes organizational, social, and ethical standards and values in the conduct of internal as well as external business activities.

Interpersonal Sensitivity

Deals with others in a manner that shows a capacity to understand and respond appropriately to their needs.

Intuition

Uses hunch, feel, 'sixth sense' to identify issues and possible solutions.

Learning Ability

Assimilates and applies new, job-related information in a timely manner.

Listening

Draws out opinions and information from others in face-to-face interaction.

Negotiating

Communicates information and/or arguments effectively, gains support and acceptance of other parties and compromises when appropriate.

Numerical Reasoning

Analyzes, interprets and evaluates complex numerical as well as statistical information, arriving at logical deductions and conclusions.

Oral Communication

Expresses thoughts effectively and convincingly, using appropriate verbal and non-verbal behaviour to reinforce the content of the message.

Performance Orientation

Is concerned to optimize the effective and efficient management of available resources.

Personal Impact

Creates a positive first impression, commands attention and respect, and is socially confident.

Political and Organizational Awareness

Considers probable support or opposition to ideas or action in terms of external, organizational, professional or sectional interests and constraints.

Prioritizing

Accurately assesses the relative importance of objectives, activities and events in relation to organizational goals.

Resilience

Is able to maintain high performance levels under pressure and/ or opposition and is able to maintain composure in the face of disappointments, criticism and/or rejection.

Risk Taking

Ability to stretch or go beyond personal/professional comfort, with confidence in one's own skills and abilities.

Self-awareness

Is aware of personal strengths, needs and limitations and the part they play in the exercise of effective management.

Self-confidence

Demonstrates a genuine belief in the likelihood of personal success and communicates a positive self-esteem to others.

Sociability

Is socially outgoing and able to mix easily with others.

Strategic Planning

Sets goals and objectives based on a clear vision of the future and works towards their achievement, while ensuring that short-term goals are met.

Teamwork

Co-operates with others and is able, where appropriate, to complement the roles of others by taking on the role of a leader, peer or subordinate.

Tenacity

Stays with a position or plan of action until the desired objective is achieved or is no longer reasonably attainable.

Time Management

Is able to plan and organize own use of time, meets deadlines, and does not have to rely on the last minute.

Troubleshooting

Able to gather information and quickly, accurately identify the causes of problems in work-related activities and processes.

Vision

Is able to view events and possibilities from multiple perspectives, develop future-oriented scenarios, 'helicopter' above the current situation, and see the 'bigger picture'.

Vitality

Maintains a high activity level, is enthusiastic, motivated and energetic.

Written Communication

Expresses thoughts in writing in a grammatically correct, well-organized and well-structured manner.

Table 8.1: Generic Competency Dictionary

Customer Partnership	Relationship Management	• Negotiates requirements • Manages needs and expectations • Builds effective alliances • Maintains personal contact • Uses formal and informal communication

(*contd.*)

Table 8.1(*contd.*)

		• Builds respect and trust • Follows-up with customers • Focuses on long-term relationship
	Business Focus	• Focuses on customer requirements • Finds ways to improve service • Understands client's business • Considers customer perspective • Balances technology and customer requirement • Prioritizes business requirements • Stays abreast of technology and business • Understands policies and impact
Team Collaboration	Team Building	• Inspires and motivates to excel • Articulates vision and purpose • Ensures role understanding • Delegates responsibility and authority • Recognizes efforts and results • Focuses on important elements • Creates ownership of projects • Promotes industrial accountability
	Organizational Awareness	• Accounts for impact on others • Co-ordinates with all groups • Straightforward about all issues

(*contd.*)

Table 8.1 (*contd.*)

		• Communicates with all parties • Builds relationship network • Includes relevant people • Uses collaborative problem solving • Negotiates and compromises
	Problem-Solving Skills	• Makes contingency plans • Encourages group participation • Helps without taking responsibility away • Manages teams' decision making • Helps manage conflict • Knows when to take control • Helps others understand impact • Uses group facilitation
Developing People	Respects Others	• Seeks solutions not blame • Maintains self-control • Is sensitive to other's needs • Is fair and even handed • Maintains other's self-esteem • Works with all people/levels • Listens to obtain input • Respects ideas and contributions
	On the Job Development (OJD)/Coaching	• Improves skills in team • Uses cross-training and assignments • Sets clear objectives • Assesses employee needs regularly • Is open to feedback • Uses mistakes for learning • Provides feedback • Assesses skills for projects

(*contd.*)

Table 8.1(*contd.*)

Technical Integrity	Technical expertise/ commitment	• Technologically up-to-date • Builds in testing procedures • Sets technology, vision direction • Takes a stand when right • Has strong grasp of technology • Puts in necessary effort • User-friendly communicator • Leverages/optimizes technology
	Project/Quality Management	• Accepts full responsibility • Anticipates problems • Communicates project status to all • Breaks projects down • Juggles multiple projects • Stays on goals regardless • Uses resources effectively • Drives quality and standards

Rating/Scale of Competencies

Various rating scales can be used (see Chapter Two and Case Examples in Part Two of the book). Below is another example of rating the behavioural indicators of various competencies.

When an organization decides to develop a competency framework or model, the question arises that what should be the criteria? Below is listed a comprehensive range of performance criteria that have been drawn from job analysis and performance review process in a variety of organizations inclusive of MNCs, Indian corporates and public sector. The list can be reviewed along with the definition and then prioritized according to how best they reflect the criteria most significant for managerial and leadership excellence.

Further, it can be rated on a 1–6 point scale, showing the degree to which each of the criteria below is critical for the success:

1. Must have
2. Very important
3. Important
4. Not particularly important
5. Little importance
6. Not important at all

Once the competencies have been defined they can be clustered together under broader perspectives and the behavioural indicators are defined as shown in Table 8.2.

Table 8.2: Behavioural Ratings of Various Competencies—An Example

	Depth of knowledge	Quality Conscious	Supervision	Time Management	Leadership	Innovation
Beginner	Familiarity with basic concepts.	Meets basic quality requirements.	High level of supervision expected, every stage monitored to ensure quality. Detailed procedures and guidelines available to describe work steps.	Typically, goes through a learning curve starting from scratch. Able to deliver within reasonable time in simple situations.	Expected to lead innovation within span of activities.	Minor process/work step improvements.
Intermediate	Thoroughly understands fundamental concepts and their application in the field of knowledge.	Above level of the quality which satisfies organizational output requirements.	Output monitored/supervised. Output quality defined to ensure adherence to standards of delivery.	Up the learning curve and can therefore crash learning time. Permitted to experiment and learn quickly to get it right.	Lead innovation in teams.	Ability to improve methods/approaches to demonstrate significant benefits.
Advanced	Thoroughly understands advanced concepts and their application in the field of knowledge.	High quality output delighting clients/customers and setting new benchmarks for the organization.	Directionally monitored, provided significant freedom to determine quality and level of outputs.	Get it right first time on most occasions. Some leeway granted for gaining familiarity with situation/environment.	Expected to be an authority and lead innovation in the organization.	Brings in new ideas which are radically different from existing methods/approaches.
Expert	Very deep understanding of and on the cutting edge of R&D/involved in path breaking.	Flawless, exemplary work, setting aspiration targets for others to emulate.	Is a guide for others. Approached by others for evaluating/criticizing their output.	Gets it right the first time every time. No space for learning. Expected to deliver based on inherent expertise.	Globally recognized thought to be a leader.	Paradigm shift in approach/method.

CHAPTER NINE

Generic Competency Model for Leadership Role in any Organization

Competency Clusters for General Leadership Model

The competencies within the dictionary have been grouped into the following four clusters: Thinking Capabilities, Leadership Effectiveness, Self-management and Social Awareness. Each cluster covers a broad range of behaviours and provides an overall picture of focus of different behaviours.

- **Thinking Capabilities:** This cluster captures the behaviours associated with problem solving and planning, as well as one's cognitive ability to research, analyze and make well-thoughtout decisions which are aligned to the organization's strategic direction.
- **Leadership Effectiveness:** This cluster groups leadership qualities and behaviours that allow one to have an impact on their employee's contribution, development and understanding of their role. In addition, this cluster draws on behaviours associated with one's ability to align others to the organization's vision.
- **Self-management:** This cluster includes the competencies related to one's ability to know one's own triggers, preferences

and internal resources and be able to apply those to guide one's performance.

- **Social Awareness:** This cluster includes the competencies related to one's ability to manage the relationships effectively. This cluster also draws on behaviours associated with being socially aware of the work environment and how best to make an impact.

Box 9.1: Generic Competency Model for Leadership Role

Thinking Capabilities
- Decisiveness
- Strategic Orientation

Leadership Effectiveness
- Development of People
- Team Leadership

Self-management
- Achievement Orientation
- Self-confidence/Courage of Convictions

Social Awareness
- Impact and Influence
- Relationship Building

Thinking Capabilities

1. Decisiveness: Decisiveness is the ability to make decisions based on an analysis of the information presented in the face of ambiguous or conflicting situations, or when there is an associated risk.

Behavioural Indicators

- Makes and implements decisions where necessary information is available and the stakeholders share compatible objectives.
- Recognizes conflicting situations as they arise and determines appropriate responses.
- Takes ownership of decisions and ensures decisions are consistent with legislation, precedent and established policies/procedures.

- Implements ideas and approaches that are likely to add value, but may not work out.
- Puts systems in place to proactively monitor risks and determine acceptable risk tolerances.
- Champions initiatives with significant potential paybacks, but possible adverse consequences, based on an assessment of the risks, benefits, impacts, etc.
- Integrates risk management into programme management and organizational planning.

2. Strategic Orientation: Strategic orientation is the ability to link long-range visions and concepts to daily work. It implies the ability to think conceptually and to 'see the big picture'. It includes an understanding of the capabilities, nature and potential of the department and the organization. It involves taking calculated risks based on an awareness of socio-economic and political issues as they impact the strategic direction of the department and the organization.

Behavioural Indicators

- Is able to analyze and comprehend operational as well as organizational goals and strategies developed by others.
- Uses understanding of business fundamentals to add value at meetings.
- Prioritizes work in alignment with business goals, acts and implements strategies and policies in accordance with the organization's strategies, objectives and goals.
- Projects or thinks about long-term applications of current activities.
- Anticipates reactions to different initiatives.
- Actively increases one's own knowledge/awareness of the business and competitive environment to determine long-term issues, problems or opportunities.
- Develops and establishes broad scale, longer-term objectives, goals or projects (e.g., affecting a department, several departments or the organization).
- Considers how present policies, processes and methods might be affected by future developments and trends.

- Ensures contingency plans exist for problems and situations that might occur.
- Redesigns the structure and/or operations of the department or organization to better meet long-term objectives.
- Establishes a course of action to accomplish a long-term goal and shares with others his/her personal view of the desirable future state of the organization.

Leadership Effectiveness

1. Development of People: Development of people involves taking actions to develop people's contribution and potential. Involves a genuine intent to foster the long-term learning or development of others, including direct reports, peers, team members or other staff. The focus is on the developmental intent and effect rather than on a formal role of training.

Behavioural Indicators

- Expresses positive expectations about an employee's potential even when others might not share the same beliefs about that person's potential.
- Offers suggestions that help people find solutions to their problems.
- Asks questions, gives tests or uses other methods to verify that others have understood explanation or directions.
- Gives feedback to direct reports, peers and/or team members or other staff in behavioural rather than personal terms for developmental purposes, and refers them to available resources to help further their success.
- Documents and follows through on a specific development plan for direct reports to support the achievement of performance targets and competencies.
- Arranges appropriate and helpful assignments, formal training or other experiences, for the purpose of fostering a person's learning and development (may include career pathing or career planning).
- Understands and identifies a training or developmental need and establishes new programmes or materials to meet it.

- Actively supports competent employees in seeking lateral and promotional opportunities to further their career.

2. Team Leadership: Team leadership is the intention to take a role as leader in a team or other group. Leadership involves communicating a compelling vision and embodying the values of the organization. Team leadership is generally, but not always, shown from a position of formal authority. The 'team' here should be understood broadly as any group in which the person takes on a leadership role, including the organization as a whole.

Behavioural Indicators

- Makes sure the group has all the necessary information.
- Matches the skills of the individual to the requirements of the work.
- Anticipates the implications of project changes on resource needs.
- Gets others' input for purposes of promoting the effectiveness of the group or process. Resolves conflicts in the team, gives fair feedback (individual or collective), etc.
- Acts to build team spirit for purposes of promoting the effectiveness of the group or process.
- Recognizes staff efforts by celebrating accomplishments.
- Takes a proactive, positive view of the staff and their capabilities, ensuring they understand their role and responsibilities, counselling and supporting them in improving their skills.
- Fosters a climate of openness, trust and solidarity among the staff by treating each person as a valued team member where people feel comfortable in expressing their opinions and needs.
- Sets a good example by personally modelling desired behaviour and establishing norms for group behaviour 'rules of engagement'; takes appropriate action if group norms are violated.
- Takes action to ensure that others buy into the leader's mission, goals, agenda, climate, tone and policy.
- Inspires confidence in the mission.
- Generates excitement, enthusiasm and commitment to the group mission.

Self-management

1. Achievement Orientation: Achievement orientation involves working to achieve results and improve individual as well as organizational contribution. It is a concern for working well or for surpassing a standard of excellence. The standard may be one's own past performance (striving for improvement); an objective measure (results orientation); outperforming others (competitiveness); challenging goals one has set; or trying something new that will improve organizational results (innovation). Achievement orientation also involves effectively managing internal and external resources to achieve the organization's goals.

Behavioural Indicators

- Sets and achieves individual performance targets aligned with the business plan, keeping others informed of the progress or barriers to achievement.
- Identifies resources (including partnerships or indirect resourcing approaches) that will facilitate the achievement of the organization's goals.
- Keeps track of and measures outcomes against a standard of excellence not imposed by others.
- Makes specific changes in the system or in own work methods to improve performance (examples may include doing something better, faster, at lower cost, more efficiently; or improves quality, client satisfaction, morale, etc.), without setting any specific goal.
- Sets and works to meet goals that are a definite stretch, but not unrealistic or impossible. These may be goals one sets for oneself or goals one sets for direct reports.
- Sets out to achieve a unique standard. The standard may process-oriented or people related (e.g., 'No one had ever done it before').
- Analyzes organizational outcomes in order to make decisions, set priorities or choose goals on the basis of calculated inputs and outputs. This includes analyzing both process and people related outcomes.
- Provides leadership in effective management and stewardship of resources.

- Makes decisions that allocate limited resources (time, people, budgetary, etc.) to meet programme delivery and/or policy objectives.
- Knows how and when to influence policy development in order to impact policy and delivery outcomes.

2. Self-confidence/Courage of Convictions: Self-confidence/ Courage of convictions is a belief in one's own capability as expressed in increasingly challenging circumstances and confidence in one's decisions or opinions, within the framework of public interest, ethics, values and organizational integrity. It may include providing leadership, direction and inspiration to others by making difficult decisions and taking actions that may not be popular, but are in the best interests of the organization and its clients.

Behavioural Indicators

- Proposes new or modified approaches, practices and processes, defending them effectively if challenged.
- Takes on activities and projects that need to be done, even though they may not be easy or have popular support.
- Reassesses position in the face of justified or persistent resistance.
- Speaks up when in disagreement with management, clients or others, but does so tactfully, stating own view clearly and confidently, even in a conflict.
- In spite of complex challenges and no guarantees of success or reward, moves issues or change initiatives forward, on the basis of the personal conviction that it is the right thing to do.
- Acknowledges personal responsibility for outcomes from decisions made.
- Makes decisions having significant consequences that are good for the organization and consistent with the values of the organization, subject to public scrutiny.
- Instils a desire in groups of people to take action, through encouragement and positive example.

Social Awareness

1. Impact and Influence: This implies an intention to persuade, convince, influence or impress others (individuals or groups) in order to get them to go along with or to support the organization's direction. The 'key' is to understand others, since it is based on the desire to have a specific impact or effect on others where the person has his or her own agenda, a specific type of impression to make, or a course of action that he or she wants the others to adopt.

Behavioural Indicators

- Uses direct persuasion in a discussion or presentation.
- Makes no apparent attempt to adapt the presentation to the interest and level of the audience.
- Takes two or more steps to persuade, without trying to adapt specifically to the level or interest of an audience.
- Makes two or more different arguments or points in a presentation or a discussion.
- Adapts a presentation or discussion to appeal to the interest and level of others.
- Anticipates the effect of an action or other details on people's image of the speaker.
- Anticipates and prepares for others' reactions.
- Takes two or more steps to influence, with each step adapted to the specific audience.
- Builds 'behind-the-scenes' support, for ideas.
- Uses an in-depth understanding of the interactions within a group to move toward a specific agenda (e.g., may withhold information to have specific effects).

2. Relationship Building: Relationship building involves the ability to develop contacts and relationships, internal and external to the organization, to facilitate work efforts or to gain support/co-operation. It implies building long-term or on-going relationships with clients or stakeholders (e.g., someone internal or external to the organization, on whom your work has an impact). This type of relationship is often quite deliberate and is typically focused on the way the relationship is conducted.

Behavioural Indicators

- Makes or sustains informal contacts with others in addition to contacts required in the course of work (such as unstructured or spontaneous talks about work-related issues, children, sports, news, etc.).
- Looks for and seizes opportunities to expand one's network of key contacts and nurture the ones in place.
- Identifies key stakeholder contacts in the organization with whom a relationship must be established.
- Develops and cultivates effective working relationships with others to accomplish tasks.
- Builds a reservoir of goodwill; exchanges information, services or time with one's network.
- Initiates or participates in parties, outings, or special gatherings designed to improve or strengthen relationships with others.
- Matches staff to appropriate stakeholder contacts and co-ordinates between the contacts.
- Develops new ways to reach out to clients and stakeholders, to stimulate input and exchange of information.
- Develops and maintains a planned network of relationships with clients, internal colleagues, stakeholders and colleagues in other departments and non-government organizations.
- Uses this network to identify opportunities and gather market intelligence.
- Develops a network and taps into their expertise to seek input to problems and to find alternative ways of resolving an impasse.

Leadership Assessment Questions

Key questions add perspective as the manager assesses an individual's development needs and potential.

Will this person:

- Develop fast enough to keep up with the rest of the team?
- Take ownership of his or her problems?

Does this person:

- Have the appropriate sense of urgency?
- Have enough experience to take the next job?
- Have the stature of a senior executive?
- Have the skills or credibility to be a senior executive?

Can this person:

- Make tough people decisions that may be necessary to build the organization?
- Build a team?
- Make the transition from a staff to a line role or from a thinking to an implementation role?
- Recover from a bad or slow start?
- Develop a successor?
- Handle the increased administrative load of this position?
- Learn to conduct business more smoothly and effectively?
- Change management styles from 'tough leader' to 'coach'?
- Move to a new functional area or line of business?
- Manage unstructured people or functions?
- Develop executive perspective?
- Let go? Can he or she let direct reports assume accountability?
- Learn to effectively deal with top management? Can he or she learn to manage up? Can this person influence or manage the boss?
- Have the ability to be effective with less budget, less support or a leaner staff?
- Constructively leverage outside resources?
- Manage as well as perform functional tasks growing beyond being a personal producer and become more than a technician?
- Really move the business?
- Learn to set higher standards?
- Operate as a stand-alone executive set?
- Adjust to the organizational culture ser?

Is this person:

- Really in the right function, career track or position?
- Willing to assume a hands-on role?
- Willing to take a more aggressive leadership position?
- In the right business unit?

Leadership Assessment is a tool used to consolidate the review of individuals in a group, department, organization or business unit. In the preparation of this matrix, the manager would focus on the distribution of employees in each quadrant. The manager would consider:

- Are the right people in the right jobs, performing at maximum levels?
- Is this the mix of personnel necessary to drive the business?
- How does this mix of results and behaviour compare with the mix of previous review periods?
- Who needs to be reassigned to another position to improve results and/or behaviours?
- Does anyone need to be outplaced?
- Who could be promoted to further realize career and organizational potential?

Leadership Assessment Matrix

Embedded in the leadership assessment is an assessment of potential. The ratings and definitions are:

- High Potential—This individual is capable of having two or more assignments with significantly greater scope and responsibility. This is an individual whose career should be carefully tracked and managed.
- Promotable—This individual is capable of having one or more assignment with significantly greater scope and responsibility.
- Experienced Professional—This individual has demonstrated depth and capabilities, which reflect his or her expertise. This

professional coaches those less experienced and less knowledgeable and is a skilled professional who may be moved to other positions, though the move is likely to be at the same level of responsibility.

Reassess Potential—This individual is yet to demonstrate the capabilities. It may be, he has been in the company for less than six months or needs to be moved from his present assignment. He may be reassigned or outplaced and if he is close to retirement, he may not be recommended for any future positions.

CHAPTER TEN

Competency Model for HR

THE competency model for HR is developed for various positions—HR Head, HR Manager and HR Executive. All the HR functions have been taken into consideration and the model is based on the findings from 18 organizations across all sectors. The model can be easily put to use or customized without much effort, considering the range of functions being handled by the position holder.

Human Resource Head

The Human Resource Head leads a team of human resource professionals and administrative staff in the delivery of a full range of HR functions. These include labour relations, succession management, staffing, classification, recruitment initiatives, workplace diversity, HR planning, organization development and job as well as organizational design.

As the Head, one has to establish and foster a culture, building strong working relationships within the organization. Working closely with the team, ensure that needs are met, issues are addressed and situations are managed in a collaborative, consultative, creative and flexible manner.

One has to continuously enhance the process and be a part of the business plan. Competency model for HR Head has 11 competencies, as given in Box 10.1, all of which are important for superior performance.

Box 10.1: Competency Model for HR Head

- Strategic Thinking
- Business Acumen
- Relationship Building and Networking
- Team Leadership and Development
- Results Orientation
- Impact and Influence
- Communication
- Personal Effectiveness
- Internal Customer Orientation
- Human Resources Expertise
- Change Leadership

Strategic Thinking

Understands interactions with the external world, including broader implications and longer term impacts and risks; contributes to the development of the organization's vision and long-term strategy; determines actions that will achieve desirable outcomes.

Behavioural Indicators

- Knowledge of human resource issues, challenges and their impact on human resource management.
- Knowledge of human resource management practices, including strategies to recruit, support and sustain a diverse workforce. (Corporate Statement)
- Ability to understand and clearly articulate the implication and impact of human resource challenges as well as develop and implement strategies that will achieve desirable outcomes.

Business Acumen

Demonstrates an understanding of organizational direction, culture, business challenges, priorities and needs; takes action to ensure that the HR functions are aligned with business direction and needs.

Behavioural Indicators

- Knowledge of the organization's and the department's strategic direction, programmes, services, environmental influences and their long-term impact as it relates to human resource management.
- Ability to understand and clearly articulate the direction, culture, business challenges and priorities of the organization and take the appropriate action to align these functions with business direction and needs.

Relationship Building and Networking

Continuously works to build and maintain critical relationships and networks of contacts that contribute to the achievement of goals.

Behavioural Indicator

- Ability to develop and maintain critical relationships and networks that contribute to the achievement of the goals of the organization.

Team Leadership and Development

Sets clear direction; uses strategies to build team morale and productivity; promotes a friendly and co-operative environment, conducive to personal and professional development; champions efforts to resolve obstacles outside of the team's direct influencing skill.

Behavioural Indicator

- Ability to develop and implement strategies that build, support and enhance team morale and productivity as well as promote a positive and co-operative work environment.

Results Orientation

Establishes and maintains effective accountability systems to review activities and goals against strategies; analyzes performance information to set priorities and take calculated risks to improve the processes and HR activities; predicts emerging issues and manages associated risks.

Behavioural Indicators

- Ability to develop and maintain effective performance management and accountability systems ensuring activities and goals support the strategy of improved client service delivery.
- Ability to accurately predict emerging issues and appropriately manage associated risks related to performance management and accountability systems.

Impact and Influence

Acts to persuade, convince or influence others in order to have specific impact or effect.

Behavioural Indicators

- Ability to persuade, convince and influence others in order to achieve understanding and reach agreement.
- Ability to develop and maintain open and honest professional relationships with colleagues, clients and stakeholders.
- Ability to guide and coach a diverse group of employees, that results in a team that can meet its goals and objectives, while maintaining a healthy, productive, respectful and safe work-environment that is free of discrimination. (Corporate Statement)

Communication

Clearly conveys and receives messages in ways which capture interest, inform and gain support; encourages input.

Behavioural Indicator

- Ability to clearly and accurately articulate and receive information that captures interest, informs and gains support.

Personal Effectiveness

Understands one's own patterns, preferences and styles under normal and stressful conditions, and their impact on others, as well as the need to modify those traits to work effectively with others.

Behavioural Indicator

- Ability to understand and recognize one's own actions and conduct under normal and stressful conditions and take steps to minimize its impact to ensure a healthy, happy work-environment.

Internal Customer Orientation

Serves the organization through focusing individual or team effort on meeting key internal customers-needs through development and implementation of sound strategies and action plan.

Behavioural Indicator

- Ability to conceptualize, develop, implement and evaluate strategies, that reflect the department's strategic plan and meet the organization's needs.

Human Resources Expertise

Knowledge of Human Resource principles, concepts and strategies, as well as current trends and issues.

Behavioural Indicator

- Knowledge of Human Resource principles, concepts, strategies, current trends and issues.

Change Leadership

Energizes and alerts groups to the need for change; takes responsibility to champion the change effort through building and maintaining support and commitment.

Behavioural Indicators

- Ability to lead, develop, champion and promote change in the workplace, building employee and departmental support and commitment.
- Ability to persuade and convince others to gain support for the recommended need for change, providing reasonable and logical options; and solutions.

Human Resource Manager

A Human Resource Manager may either be a generalist handling a variety of HR activities in a number of areas, or a specialist focused on one select function. HR managers provide advice and guidance on organizational and team development, organizational structure, job design and classification, industrial relations, recruitment, staffing and human resource planning.

A HR manager must have a clear understanding of business, focusing on achieving a high quality, strategic result for the organization. Using highly developed facilitation and interpersonal skills, HR managers contribute to client relations and business partnerships based on collaboration and respect. The Competency Model for HR Manager has been illustrated in Box 10.2.

Box 10.2: Competency Model for HR Manager

- Internal Customer
- Relationship Building
- Job Knowledge
- Knowledge of Government and Clients' Business
- Teamwork
- Results Orientation
- Impact and Influence
- Problem Solving
- Communication
- Personal Effectiveness
- Flexibility

Internal Customer

Serves the interests of colleagues by proactively focusing effort on understanding their challenges and needs, and working with them to address those needs; follows consulting principles, and uses a consultative approach and process in working.

Behavioural Indicators

- Demonstrated an ability to listen to and accurately understand the needs and challenges.

- Work with them to resolve human resource problems and issues.
- Knowledge of consulting principles and processes.

Relationship Building

Continuously works to build and maintain professional and trusting relationships, partnerships and networks of contacts to broaden information and to support the achievement of goals.

Behavioural Indicators

- Ability to build and maintain professional relationships.
- Networks to support the needs and achieve organizational goals.

Job Knowledge

Knowledge of HR principles, practices and tools (staffing, classification, learning, performance management, compensation, benefits, labour relations, team building, conflict management, change management, organizational design and development, workforce planning, facilitation, consultation).

Behavioural Indicators

- Knowledge of human resource principles, practices and tools relating to staffing, classification, learning, performance management, compensation, benefits, labour relations, team building, conflict management, change management, organizational design and development, facilitation and consultation.
- Knowledge of human resource management practices, including strategies to recruit, support and sustain a diverse workforce.
- Ability to design, develop and successfully deliver and evaluate human resource services using professional consulting skills and techniques.

Knowledge of Government and Clients' Business

Understands organizational direction, culture, business challenges, priorities and needs; aligns services with clients' business needs.

Behavioural Indicators

- Knowledge of the department's strategic direction and programmes.
- Ability to understand and clearly articulate the business direction, culture and challenges.
- Prioritizes the organizational needs and align human resource strategy to business needs.

Teamwork

Works to promote a positive climate, good morale and co-operation between team members; builds team spirit; may participate in multiple teams.

Behavioural Indicator

- Ability to develop and build a positive and professional climate that enhances good morale and co-operation between team members.

Results Orientation

Plans, manages and follows through with work projects and tasks to ensure the flow and timely completion of activities that deliver results.

Behavioural Indicator

- Ability to plan, prioritize, organize and follow through on work projects and tasks ensuring goals are accomplished in a timely manner.

Impact and Influence

Acts to influence, persuade and productively gain others' commitment to ideas and objectives.

Behavioural Indicator

- Ability to influence, persuade and gain the commitment of colleagues to new ideas and the objectives of the organization.

Problem Solving

Uses alternate and/or creative ways of looking at issues or problems and linking information to a solution; assembles ideas, issues and observations into clear and useful explanations and solutions.

Behavioural Indicators

- Ability to accurately analyze ideas, issues and observations.
- Identify and develop a variety of alternative explanations and solutions.

Communication

Presents information, ideas and questions in a clear and understandable manner; demonstrates accurate assessment and sensitivity to the behaviour of individuals and groups; takes appropriate action to respond to others.

Behavioural Indicators

- Ability to clearly articulate and present information, ideas and questions in an understandable manner verbally and in writing.
- Ability to accurately assess the behaviour of individuals and groups and take appropriate actions and make necessary changes in response to their behaviour.

Personal Effectiveness

Knows own strengths and areas for development; demonstrates time management and personal organization, commitment to learning; has the ability to use healthy coping strategies in working through change and transition.

Behavioural Indicators

- Knowledge of one's own strengths and areas for development and take appropriate action to learn and grow.
- Ability to recognize symptoms of stress in self and others and take steps to minimize its impact ensuring individual good health and organizational well-being.

Flexibility

Works effectively within a variety of situations, and with various individuals or groups; understands and appreciates different and opposing perspectives on an issue, adapting one's approach as the requirements of a situation change; able to manage multiple and diverse issues and priorities while meeting client needs.

Behavioural Indicators

- Ability to create an environment that recognizes, supports, respects and welcomes diversity of employees.
- Ability to guide and coach a diverse group of employees, that results in a team that can meet its goals and objectives, while maintaining a healthy, productive, respectful and safe work environment that is free of discrimination.
- Ability to develop, build and maintain open and honest work relationships with a challenging and diverse range of employees.
- Ability to manage and organize multiple, diverse issues and priorities that meet the needs.

Human Resource Executive

Human Resource Executive provides guidance related to HR procedures, protocols and employee information. Provides excellent employee relationships as he possesses a sound understanding of human resource practices and principles.

The HR executive supports and has a clear understanding of the HR resource professionals' expectations as well as their employee's needs. By working in collaboration with colleagues and employees, the HR executive promotes a positive climate, good morale and co-operation between team members by completing work assignments, achieving common goals and ensuring desired outcomes. The Competency Model for an HR executive is shown in Box 10.3.

Box 10.3: Competency Model for HR Executive

- Internal Customer
- Human Resource Expertise
- Teamwork
- Results Orientation
- Communication
- Personal Effectiveness

Internal Customer

Works with clients to understand their needs and to address those needs appropriately, in a timely manner.

Behavioural Indicators

- Ability to ask probing questions, listen, accurately comprehend and verbally as well as in writing, respond to clients and colleagues needs and inquiries in a timely manner.
- Ability to provide clear, concise and accurate information and explanations to a variety of people in both formal and informal settings.

Human Resource Expertise

Demonstrates solid knowledge and skills within own functional area, as well as a general understanding of HR practices.

Behavioural Indicators

- Knowledge of relevant human resource practices.
- Ability to read, understand and accurately apply relevant human resource policies and procedures.

Teamwork

Works collaboratively with others; promotes a positive climate, good morale and co-operation between team members.

Behavioural Indicators

- Ability to develop and maintain a positive climate.
- Demonstrate collaborative work relationships with colleagues.

Results Orientation

Works to achieve performance standards, expectations and desired outcomes.

Behavioural Indicators

- Ability to contribute towards a positive work environment by accurately completing work assignments.
- Achieve common goals, ensuring desired outcomes are met in a timely manner.
- Ability to identify, clarify and analyze relevant client concerns or problems.
- Provide sound options/recommendations and implement practical solutions in a timely manner.

Communication

Presents verbal and written information, ideas and questions in a clear and understandable manner; responds appropriately to others.

Behavioural Indicators

- Ability to communicate information and ideas; both verbally and in writing.
- Ask relevant questions in a clear, understandable and timely manner.

Personal Effectiveness

Knows own strengths and areas for development; demonstrates time management and personal organization, commitment to learning, ability to use healthy coping strategies in working through change and transition.

Behavioural Indicators

- Knowledge of one's own strengths and areas for development and taking appropriate action to learn and grow.
- Ability to recognize symptoms of stress in self and take steps to minimize its impact, ensuring good health and well-being.

CHAPTER ELEVEN

Leadership Competency Model for Automobile Industry

Leadership Competency Model

THE automobile sector has grown and has open challenges for employees as well as for business. Technical skills and continuous Research and Development (R&D) is of utmost importance, but which are those behavioural competencies, which will lead to superior performance. A study of eight automobile industries and an analysis of the factors that derive results at various levels of leadership, was the basis of the formation of a Leadership Competency Model for the Automobile Industry as shown in Box 11.1.

Box 11.1: Leadership Competency Model for Automobile Industry

- Visioning
- Direction and Goal Setting
- Judgement
- Holistic View
- Business and Customer Focus
- Inspiring Leadership
- Learning from Experience
- Drive to improve
- Networking
- Partnership
- People Development
- Team Working

Visioning

Has a clear vision for the business or operation; maintains a long-term, big-picture view; foresees obstacles and opportunities and generates breakthrough ideas.

Behavioural Indicators

- Develops a clear vision for the future of the business or organization.
- Conveys a clear sense of the organization's purpose and mission that captures the imagination of others.
- Maintains a long-term, big-picture view of the business and identifies the future needs and opportunities for the business.
- Recognizes when it is time to shift strategic direction and anticipates the evolution of the industry as well as how the organization must adapt to these changes in order to sustain competitive advantage.
- Sees problems and understands issues before others do.
- Challenges status-quo thinking and assumptions.
- Comes up with fresh perspectives; innovative, breakthrough ideas and new paradigms that create value in the marketplace.

Direction and Goal Setting

Sets, agrees and communicates goals, standards and performance expectations in an open, straightforward and easily understandable way.

Behavioural Indicators

- Gives clear directions to support the achievement of the set strategy.
- Has clearly defined, concrete objectives, deadlines and also conducts follow-ups.
- Delegates as much as possible, adapting to the responsibilities, motivation and interest of each individual in his/her staff.
- Deals with others openly and constructively on performance issues and is prepared to take action if performance does not change.
- Helps teams to agree and commit to extending their goals.

Judgement

Sees the big picture to identify key areas or underlying issues and to develop effective strategies.

Behavioural Indicators

- Recognizes core issues and observes discrepancies, trends and interrelationships.
- Integrates ideas and observations into concepts.
- Identifies problems and situations that are not immediately obvious to others and that are not learnt from previous experiences.

Holistic View

Understands the individuals, groups, cultures and organizations that make up the business sphere as a whole.

Behavioural Indicators

- Understands what motivates and hinders people; reads unspoken language.
- Understands interpersonal processes.
- Understands people's strengths and weaknesses.
- Understands the informal structure.
- Creates good prerequisites for ensuring effective change.
- Understands the reasons for ongoing organizational behaviour and underlying problems.
- Is aware of different cultural perspectives.

Business and Customer Focus

Keeps consistent focus on the requirements of the customer and the market.

Behavioural Indicators

- Has a clear desire to add value by always seeking to focus resources and energies on the market and on customer requirements.

- Stays informed about trends and developments beyond the immediate business area—both inside and outside the organization
- Consistently aims to take the customer into consideration at all stages of a business process.
- Thinks ahead and considers the impact and implications of actions—both internally and externally.

Inspiring Leadership

Develops and communicates a clear vision and direction for the company and desires to lead people to achieve it.

Behavioural Indicators

- Creates a relaxed, pleasant and productive atmosphere characterized by co-working and co-creativeness.
- Establishes individual involvement and ownership of objectives.
- Communicates visions clearly so that everyone sees and understands.
- Inspires people to say, 'I want to do this, I choose to do this.'
- Creates a sense of confidence and trust so that change is regarded as a contribution to the development of operations.
- Combines the requirement for renewal, development and change with the individual's need for security, reliance and stability.

Learning from Experience

Reflects on own experience and results as well as on the experience and results of others, in order to learn from them for the future.

Behavioural Indicators

- Is open to learning and to feedback.
- Is aware of and develops own skills.
- Systematically reviews projects and benchmarks against the best.
- Scans the business environment to learn from others.
- Creates a climate to learn from mistakes.
- Supports others after setbacks.

Drive to Improve

Has the desire and energy to achieve tough but realistic goals and the ability to create or grasp opportunities in order to attain 'excellence'.

Behavioural Indicators

- Is action-oriented and displays a sense of urgency.
- Shows persistence.
- Strives for new levels of performance.
- Uses considerable energy and exhibits persistence so as to achieve long-term goals.
- Creates a sense of urgency regarding the delivery of results.
- Gives and creates energy.

Networking

Identifies and builds relationships with people inside and outside the organization in order to create opportunities and do whatever is necessary to reach the set business goals.

Behavioural Indicators

- Wants to work with others to optimize synergies.
- Is able to capitalize on the resources of the organization.
- Operates in different teams.
- Is an active and effective communicator and manages information exchanges efficiently.

Partnership

Understands and builds short-term or long-term relationships with third parties, adding value to both.

Behavioural Indicators

- Works to build personal relationships with suppliers, dealers and joint-venture partners in order to maximize the benefit to all concerned.
- Works to create win-win scenarios.
- Listens actively and shows interest in interplay with other people.
- Thinks through the consequences of the organization's decisions on third parties.

People Development

Fosters the long-term development of others.

Behavioural Indicators

- Contributes to learning and development in day-to-day work.
- Provides positive or mixed feedback for the purpose of enhancing development.
- Gives negative feedback in behavioural rather than personal terms.
- Develops skills and fosters learning by demanding targets or assignments that reinforce learning.
- Grants increasing responsibility with the aim of developing and stretching people.
- Has faith in people; communicates a belief in people's ability to achieve genuine personal growth.

Team Working

Works together with others in projects and processes so as to achieve better results.

Behavioural Indicators

- Listens to and seeks information from others.
- Shares skills and expertise.
- Is active on behalf of the team.
- Puts own agenda to one side in order to work to achieve team goals.
- Acts without prejudice.
- Represents the team and supports the team's joint goals.

Experiential Sharing

Case in Point—One: Hindustan Sanitaryware & Industries Ltd.—An Experience

About HSIL

Hindustan Sanitaryware & Industries Ltd. (HSIL), the largest Indian manufacturer of sanitaryware products with a market share of

~40 per cent, was established in 1960 by the Somany Group in collaboration with Twyfords, UK. It was the first company in India to manufacture Vitreous China Sanitaryware. HSIL products are sold under the brand name 'Hindware' and 'Raasi' and their expected turnover in 2005–06 was in excess of Rs 400 crores and its current market capitalization is approximately Rs 650 crores. It has been granted the 'Selected Business Superbrand 2004–06'.

Hindustan Sanitaryware & Industries Ltd. put up its plant in Bahadurgarh in 1960 (that time it was in Punjab and not Haryana) having a very small capacity. Over the period it has become one of the largest plants for manufacturing sanitaryware, employing 1,000 people in direct employment, which generates indirect employment for more than 10,000 families. HSIL today has around 38 per cent of the market share.

The company's goods are exported all across the world including Europe, Australia, Singapore, etc., and export around 10 per cent of their production.

Forbes magazine has rated HSIL amongst the 100 best, small- and medium-sized companies in the world.

HSIL has also entered into a strategic alliance worth US $1.5 billion with Sanitec Group of Finland, Europe's No. 1 bathroom solutions company, to exclusively market their flagship brand 'Keramag' in India. This will be done through HSIL's extensive all-India sales and distribution network.

The company is increasingly focusing on newer product ranges and has already introduced 50 products in the last 18 months. The company is committed to developing eco-friendly products and an example of this is their 'dual flush' closets that save water. In-fact, HSIL was the pioneer in introducing the first genuine waterless urinal.

Objective

HSIL, on the fast track of growth felt the need to develop a competency model with an objective to increase the efficiency of the organization and integrate the HR functions and PMS to the model.

Process

The JD's, Role and Responsibilities, KRA's, Process and Quality documents of the organizations were studied, the vision and mission of the organization was understood well through long discussions with the Chairman and Managing Director, JMD and the President. Following the Mc Bers Model, the BEI were conducted for all the top 24 positions. The focus was on how can the performance be more superior, success and challenges be faced and what are the competencies required to perform the given roles and responsibilities. This was followed by continuous interaction with the top management, with an objective to link it to the future strategy and business opportunities of the organization.

Competency Mapping and Assessment Centre

Individual employees were mapped on each and every identified competency through an Assessment Centre. Each one was assessed on a five-point scale. Psychometric tests, case studies, in-basket exercises, leaderless group discussions and business simulation games were used to measure the competencies.

The individual profiles were shared with each and every employee. The developmental exercise was followed by a competency-based training programme in order to fulfil the gaps identified.

After the successful completion of Phase I, Phase II comprising of middle-level managers was conducted.

The given model was developed for the various positions (Table 11.1 is the example of the competency model for the Regional Manager) along with the ratings, where '5' is excellent and '1' is below average. The competencies were divided into vital and important competencies. Important competencies are those, which are essential for the particular position whereas vital competencies are those, which are needed for critical success. The individual rating were summarized by 'Potential Mapping' that indicated the potential of an employee, where he stands today and his potential for future growth.

The model was gradually integrated in the various HR functions. The selection process and the training programmes were both competency based.

Case in Point—Two: HPCL—An Experience

About HPCL

Hindustan Petroleum Corporation Limited (HPCL) is among the leading public sector oil refining and marketing companies in

Table 11.1: Competency Model for Regional Manager

Competencies	1	2	3	4	5
Vital Competencies					
Analysis and judgement Seeks all relevant information; identifies problems, relates relevant data and identifies causes; assimilates numerical data accurately and makes sensible interpretations; work is precise and methodical, and relevant details are not overlooked; makes decisions based on logical assumption that reflect factual information.					
Product and job knowledge Ability to understand the business goals and objectives and keeps abreast of developments in the concerned area, both in the organization and external market.					
Result-oriented Sets demanding goals for self and for others; is dissatisfied with average performance; makes full use of own time and resources; sees a task through to completion, irrespective of obstacles and setbacks.					
Planning and organizing Plans priorities, assignments and the allocation of resources; organizes resources efficiently and effectively, delegating work to the appropriate staff.					

(contd.)

Table 11.1 (contd.)

Competencies	1	2	3	4	5

Customer orientation

Actively seeks to understand customers' requirements. Actions anticipate and pre-empt requests for service, based on well-developed relationships.

External awareness

Has extensive knowledge of issues and changes within the external environment and is able to identify existing or potential strengths, weaknesses, opportunities and threats to the organization. Understands the effects and implications of external factors on own decisions.

Negotiation skills

When negotiating, communicates proposals effectively, identifies a basis for compromise and reaches an agreement with others through personal power and influence.

Communication

Effectively assimilates information points and ideas clearly, is enthusiastic and lively, tailors content to audience's level of understanding, listens dispassionately and conveys the clear impression that key points have been recalled and taken into account.

Team Building

Gives clear direction and leads from the front whenever necessary. Fosters effective team working by involving subordinates' and adopting the appropriate leadership style to achieve the team's goals. Effectively monitors and evaluates the results of subordinates' work and provides feedback and advice whenever possible.

Important Competencies

Business sense
Identifies those opportunities, which will increase the organization's sales or profits; selects and exploits those activities which will result in the largest returns.

Creativity/innovation
Produces highly imaginative and innovative ideas and proposals, which are not obvious to less perceptive colleagues.

Change-oriented
Actively seeks to change the job and environment whenever appropriate. Is proactive, encourages the introduction of new structures, methods and procedures.

India with a turnover of Rs 76,920 crores in the year 2005–06. The HPCL infrastructure includes a fuels/lube refinery with a capacity of 5.5 million tonnes at Mumbai and a fuels refinery with a capacity of 7.5 million tonnes at Visakh. Its marketing network includes 37 terminals/TOPs, 92 depots, 40 LPG bottling plants, seven lube blending plants, 13 aviation service facilities, 21 lube depots and cross country product pipelines between Mumbai and Pune and between Visakh–Vijaywada–Secunderabad, which service HPCL's retail outlets, Superior Kerosene Oil/Light Diesel Oil and LPG dealerships spread across the country. The driving force behind these giant operations are more than 10 thousand employees.

Consequent to the economic liberalization measures introduced in the country in the mid-1990s, the corporation commissioned a Business Process Re-engineering (BPR) study to review the corporation's long-term strategy, IT strategy and its HR practices. As a result of this study, the corporation was restructured on product line basis into Strategic Business Units (SBUs) with the required delegation of authorities. While the above organizational changes have helped to sustain its market position and revenue, a need was felt to upgrade, revitalize and renew management quality to bring in a more vibrant, winning and cohesive organization to meet the challenges posed by continuously increasing competition and customer expectations ushered in by the deregulation of the market.

The corporation undertook major business and HR initiatives including Organization Transformation, Competency Mapping and Development Centre (CM & DC) and Balanced Scorecard.

Under the CM & DC process, in collaboration with its implementation partner, HPCL developed Behavioural Competency Framework (BCF) based on which multiple development centres for various levels of management have been conducted.

Simultaneously, the generic Technical Competency Framework (TCF) for all major job families have been developed.

Objective

The objective of the Competency Mapping and Development Centre Project was to build-up human capabilities to match the needs of the business of tomorrow through the development of deep understanding, internal expertise and applications of competency mapping, assessment and development processes.

Behavioural Competency Frames at HPCL

Individual Contributor Frame

An individual was assessed on five competencies under the Individual Contributor Frame as shown in Box 11.2.

Box 11.2: Competency Model—HPCL

Sl. No.	Competencies
1.	Dynamic Customer Focus
2.	Active Learning and Agility
3.	Co-operative Teamwork
4.	Enduring Commitment and Initiative
5.	Drive for Excellence

Process

Six tools were used to assess the individuals on the given five competencies. Each competency was assessed through two or more tools and each tool measured more than one competency. The tools used were psychometric test, group discussion, in-basket interviews, team simulation, simulation presentation, role play and competency-based structured interview. There were 3:1 assessors. The competency profile was shared with each and every employee in a one to one session. This was followed by the Individual Development Plan (IDP) Form.

Each employee was supposed to have selected at least two competencies from the opportunity/development area. The list of possible projects to be undertaken was discussed in the group along with HPCL officers. The individual plans and projects were also discussed with the employees and were laid down at the time of individual sessions. A sample report is shown which summarizes Competency Profile along with opportunity areas and areas of development in Box 11.3 and Individual Development Plan Form in Box 11.4.

Box 11.3: Competency Profile—HPCL

Competency						
Dynamic Customer Focus	Active Learning and Agility	Co-operative Teamwork	Enduring Commitment and Initiative	Drive for Excellence	Overall Rating	
						D
						D+
						C
						C+
						B
						B+
						A
						A+

(A Sample)

Opportunity Areas	Areas of Development
Dynamic customer focus	Drive for excellence
Enduring commitment and initiative	Co-operative teamwork
	Active learning and agility

Developmental Need Identification Report (A Sample)

Introduction

This report provides a description of the strengths and developmental needs as observed during the Developmental Need Identification Programme in New Delhi.

It is important for HPCL to grow and develop leadership talent internally. Therefore, in order to keep the leadership pipeline at HPCL

Box 11.4: Individual Development Plan Form (A Sample)

1. Name of the Participant :
2. Designation :
3. Location :
4. Name of the Supervisor :
5. Supervisor's Designation :

Developmental Tools that I will use to build upon competencies

Name of the Competency:

Development tools	Action steps to be taken by employee	Target completion date	Progress indicator/Result	Others involved	Nature of support needed from others

Signature of Participant

Date _____

well-supplied with individuals who are growing their abilities to lead, the business simulation of this developmental programme was created with the goal of presenting participants with challenges similar to those they are likely to face as employees. This development progamme was designed to capture individual competencies. You participated in a business simulation with a number of challenges. The focus was on the overall impact of your efforts and behaviours and their effect on the organization. Therefore, your feedback focuses on the behaviours exhibited during the programme rather than on 'right or wrong' responses to the situations and tasks presented. This report comprises of your responses during the various activities along with the psychometric test.

Definitions Used

Overall Score:

A+: Demonstrates **excellence in all competencies** with a very high frequency/consistency.

A: Demonstrates **very strong capabilities** in **most behavioural indicators of all competencies**.

B+: Demonstrates **strong capabilities** in **several behavioural indicators of most competencies** and is considered the 'right fit' for the current role.

B: Demonstrates well developed capabilities in **some behavioural indicators** of **several competencies**.

C+: Demonstrates **well developed capabilities in some** and **above average capabilities in remaining competencies** in a consistent manner.

C: Demonstrates **average** capabilities in most competencies in a **consistent manner**.

D+: Demonstrates average capabilities in most competencies but **not in a consistent manner**.

D: **Does not demonstrate expected behaviour** across most/ all competencies of the current profile.

HPCL has so far successfully integrated the Competency Mapping process to the following areas of HR:

(a) Recruitment/Absorption process/Performance Appraisal of Officer Trainees

(A Sample)

Competency: Dynamic Customer Focus

Definition: Demonstrates concern for meeting changing customer needs in a manner that provides customer satisfaction.

D	D+	C	C+	B	B+	A	A+

His work pace should facilitate his ability to champion or deliver customer-focused initiatives and activities. His assertive nature should help him to effectively advocate customer-focused initiatives and activities. His interest in analyzing people should help him to recognize their perspective and adapt his approach to better influence them. This should help him to align business offerings with customer needs.

Demonstrated evidences:

In-Basket (Tool 1)

He demonstrated the concern for meeting customer needs that lead to customer satisfaction by giving high priority to the letter of complaint.

Creativity (Simulation Presentation) (Tool 2)

He symbolized pictures well. He could have demonstrated analyzing data on customer needs and awareness of the market trends and competitors information. His approach is traditional.

Role Play (Tool 3)

He should have listened and acted on suggestions and feedback of the colleagues. He gathered and analyzed data on customer dissatisfaction. Could not demonstrate awareness of the market trends and competitors' information.

Somewhat cautious and skeptical in his view of others, he may not trust customer intentions. Concerned that they may take excess advantage, he may be reticent to suggestions and feedback given by customers.

(b) Behavioural/Technical Trainings

(c) Multi-rater feedback system

(d) Promotions from Non-Executive to Executive cadre

The recruitment of Officer Trainees (OT) in the year 2005 was based on the Behavioural competencies of HPCL. The panel of internal interviewers were trained on 'Behavioural Event Interviews' and accordingly around 300 candidates were recruited into the Corporation based on BEI methodology (apart from usual written test, group discussions, etc.). Further, these Officer Trainees were subjected to technical competency written test at the end of their training period, which was a prerequisite for their absorption into the Corporation.

At HPCL, all the training programmes are designed and delivered basis the respective competency frameworks, be it behavioural or technical.

HPCL has also initiated multi-rater feedback system to some of their outstanding achievers and key position holders. The entire feedback has been designed basis the Behavioural Competency dictionaries of HPCL. These feedbacks will supplement the Development Centre outputs and encourage the individuals to build and work on their 'Individual Development Plans'.

The organizations who would like to venture into Competency development initiative, should focus more on 'Communication'. HPCL's communication strategy includes periodical communication by the way of brochures, mails from top management, a separate website for the purpose, core team's visits to various locations and conducting 'awareness workshops' linking various HR initiatives.

HPCL is actively consolidating the initiatives taken so far and getting ready to make newer forays into implementation of contemporary HR practices in line with business requirements. The competency development process is focused on internalization of the process, smoother implementation and successful linkages to various HR processes, more importantly involvement of line functionaries in all the aspects of process.

Outsourcing of such an initiative becomes important because of the expertise required at various stages but until and unless it is a drive from the top, success cannot be achieved.

Case in Point—Three: GHCL—An Experience

About GHCL

Gujarat Heavy Chemicals Limited (GHCL) is one of the premier companies in heavy chemicals and textile. GHCL was commissioned in March 1988 and over the years it has diversified into the fields of manufacturing industrial chemicals and textiles. The products are catering to both the domestic and international markets.

GHCL is distinguished by its growth, financial performance and outstanding people and processes. It is a customer-focused company committed to leadership through quality. It strives for building trusting relationships, encouraging entrepreneurship and sharing prosperity.

Objective

With a vision to meet the challenges of the national and international market, it was decided to enhance the operational performance and further develop the potentials of their employees. One of the most challenging tasks was to assess the present competencies and find out gaps for future superior performance. In order to achieve the goal, a competency mapping assignment was carried out by the author.

Competency Mapping Assignment at GHCL included the middle- and senior-level executives from DGM and above (officers at Noida, Ahmedabad, Virawal, Madurai and Vapi).

Process

A competency model for various positions, definition of all competencies along with a weighing scale were developed in Phase I and Phase II as shown in Box 11.5. The competencies were identified on the basis of discussion with the top management, in order to understand the vision and mission of GHCL including both the short-term and long-term perspective. This was followed by one to one behaviour event interviews for the position holders and the peer group that was to develop the competency model.

The draft competency model was discussed at various stages with the top management and HR for valuable inputs and these were incorporated in the model before carrying out the assessment centre.

The tools were developed and customized for the assessment centre to map the competencies of each and every individual. Two psychometric tests were also included in the battery of tools for the assessment centre.

The assessment centre was conducted at various locations.

Box 11.5: Competency Model—GHCL

Sl. No.	Competencies
1	Strategy and Direction
2	Building Global and Strategic Perspective
3	Demonstrating Business Savvy and Decisiveness
4	Leading Change and Creativity
5	Builds Collaborative Partnerships
6	Builds Organizational Capability and Inspires
7	Active Learning and Agility
8	Business Acumen
9	Manages Performances and Develops Others
10	Promoting Synergetic Teamwork
11	Decisiveness
12	Manage Execution

The individual profile of each and every participant has been prepared as an outcome of the assessment centre, which includes Rating Description, Individual Profile, Individual Competency Behavioural Summary, Competency Rating Summary, Individual Development Plan and Potential Mapping.

The desired weightages on each and every competency for various positions as well as the assessed weightages as that resulted from the assessment centre, were summarized.

A detailed potential mapping of each and every participant was given in the individual profiles. The 'potential mapping' of each individual profile summarized and gave indicates those performing indicative remarks whether the performance is beyond. His or her role to take up higher responsibility in the future or he/she is the right fit or the gaps identified to be the right fit for the role. **However, while taking a decision the past performance, consistency and the organization's requirements were also to be considered.**

Competency Model

1. Strategy and Direction

Defining how a common vision/mission will be implemented and aligning all the involved parties to reach the same goals and objectives.

2. Building Global and Strategic Perspective

Develops and implements comprehensive and realistic strategies by utilizing knowledge of global and industry-wide business trends.

3. Demonstrating Business Savvy and Decisiveness

Utilizes understanding of business drivers to take courageous decisions that provide a competitive advantage.

4. Leading Change and Creativity

Initiates, manages and energizes change processes while encouraging new, innovative approaches.

5. Builds Collaborative Partnerships

Builds co-operative partnerships both internally and externally leveraging relations to meet organizational objectives within the framework of governance, policies and guidelines of the organization.

6. Builds Organizational Capability and Inspire

Works to cultivate positive relationships with others in order to drive business results and increase job satisfaction in the workplace.

7. Active Learning and Agility

Pursues new knowledge for improvement and operates from a commercial mindset, promoting the best interests of business.

8. Business Acumen

Taking a business perspective when making decisions and being aware of the impact on cash flow, company viability, service, quality and customer relations. Formulating, tracking and executing budget plans, identifying opportunities for business. Identifying, assessing and managing risk vis-à-vis pay-off/reward.

9. Manages Performance and Develops Others

Skill to communicate the performance management processes and manage performance. Makes every effort to develop both on and off the job the knowledge, skills and competencies required by a team or an individual to advance their careers.

10. Promoting Synergestic Teamwork

Provides direction and support, building co-operation while leading a team to accomplish desired objectives.

11. Decisiveness

Being able to decide in a timely manner, by bringing together a wide range of considerations and perspectives to issues, ensuring that thorough analysis is part of the decision-making process.

12. Manage Execution

Being able to reach pre-defined objectives efficiently.

Glossary of Terms

A

Accept: To receive with consent; to take without protest.

Accountability: The state of being subject to judgement for an action or result which a person has been given authority and responsibility to perform.

Act: To exert one's power so as to bring about a result; to carry out a plan or purpose. See *Execute*, *Implement* and *Perform*.

Add: To affix or attach; to find the sum of figures.

Administer: To direct the application, execution, use or general conduct of.

Adopt: To take and apply or put into action.

Advise: To give recommendations. See *Propose* and *Recommend*. To offer an informed opinion based on specialized knowledge.

Affirm: To confirm or ratify.

Align: To arrange or form in a line.

Amend: To change or modify.

Analyze: To study the factors of a situation or problem in order to determine the outcome or solution; to separate or distinguish the parts of a process or situation so as to discover their true relationships.

Anticipate: To foresee events, trends, consequences or problems in order to deal with them in advance.

Apply: To adjust or direct; to put in use.

Appraise: To evaluate as to quality, status or effectiveness of.

Approve: To sanction officially; to accept as satisfactory; to ratify, thereby assuming responsibility for (used only in the situation where the individual has final authority).

Arrange: To place in proper or desired order; to prepare for an event. See *Prepare*.

Ascertain: To find out or learn with certainty.

Assemble: To collect or gather together in a predetermined order or pattern. See *Collect*, *Compile* and *Co-ordinate*.

Assign: To give specific duties to others to perform. See *Delegate*.

Assist: To lend aid or support in some undertaking or effort. (No authority over the activity is implied.)

Assume: To take upon oneself; to undertake; to take for granted.

Assure: To confirm; to make certain of. See *Ensure*.

Attach: To bind, fasten, tie or connect.

Attend: To be present for the purpose of listening or contributing.

Audit: To examine and review a situation, condition or practice, and conclude with a detailed report on the findings.

Authority: The power to influence or command thought, opinion or behaviour.

Authorize: To empower; to permit; to establish by authority.

B

Balance: To arrange or prove so that the sum of one group equals the sum of another.

Batch: To group into a quantity for one operation.

C

Calculate: To ascertain by mathematical processes; to reckon by exercise of practical judgement.

Cancel: To strike or cross out.

Carry: To convey through the use of the hands.

Centre: To place or fix at or around the centre; to collect to a point.

Chart: To draw or exhibit in a graph.

Check: To examine for a condition; to compare for verification. See *Control*, *Examine*, *Inspect*, *Monitor* and *Verify*.

Circulate: To distribute in accordance with a plan. See *Disseminate*.

Classify: To separate into groups having systematic relations.

Clear: To get the agreement or disagreement of others.

Close: To terminate or shutdown.

Code: To transpose words or figures into symbols or characters. Also *Encode*.

Collaborate: To work or act jointly with others.

Collate: To bring together in a predetermined order.

Collect: To gather facts or data; to assemble; to accumulate. See *Assemble* and *Compile*.

Compile: To collect into a volume; to compose out of materials from other documents.

Compose: To make up, fashion or arrange.

Concur: To agree with a position, statement, act or opinion.

Conduct: To lead, guide or command the efforts of others towards producing a chore or task or goal.

Consolidate: To combine separate items into a single whole.

Construct: To set in order mentally; to arrange.

Consult: To seek advice of others; to confer.

Control: To exert power over in order to guide or restrain; to measure, interpret and evaluate for conformance with plans or expected results.

Co-operate: To work jointly with others. See *Collaborate*.

Co-ordinate: To bring into common action or condition so as to harmonize by regulating, changing, adjusting or combining. See *Assemble*.

Copy: To transfer or reproduce information.

Correct: To rectify; to make right.

Correlate: To establish a mutual or reciprocal relationship; to put in relation to each other.

Cross foot: To add across, horizontally.

Cross off: To line out, strike out.

Cross out: To eliminate by lining out.

D

Date stamp: To affix or note a date by stamping.

Decide: To choose from among alternatives or possibilities so as to end debate or uncertainty.

Delegate: To entrust to the care or management of another; to authorize or empower another to act in one's place. See *Assign*, *Authorize* and *Represent*.

Delegation: Assigning to a subordinate the responsibility and commensurate authority to accomplish an objective or specific result.

Delete: To erase; to remove.

Design: To conceive and plan in the mind for a specific use; to create, fashion, execute or construct according to a plan. See *Develop*, *Devise*, *Formulate* and *Plan*.

Determine: To make a decision; to bring about; to cause; to decide and set limits to, thereby fixing definitely and unalterably. To find out something not before known as a result of an intent to find definite and precise truth.

Develop: To conceive and create; to make active, available or usable; to set forth or make clear, evident or apparent.

Development: The result of developing.

Devise: To come up with something new, especially by combining known ideas or principles. See *Design*, *Develop*, *Formulate* and *Plan*.

Direct: To lead, guide or command the efforts of others towards producing a chosen result. See *Conduct*, *Manage* and *Supervise*.

Direction: Guidance or supervision of others.

Disassemble: To take apart.

Discover: To find out something not known before as a result of chance, exploration or investigation. See *Ascertain* and *Determine*.

Discuss: To exchange views for the purpose of convincing or reaching a conclusion.

Dissemble: To take apart.

Disseminate: To spread information or ideas. See *Circulate*, *Distribute*, *Issue* and *Release*.

Distribute: To divide or separate into classes; to pass around; to allot; to deliver to named places or persons. See *Circulate*, *Disseminate*, *Issue* and *Release*.

Divide: To separate into classes or parts, subject to mathematical division.

Draft: To compose or write papers and documents in preliminary or final form, often for the approval or clearance of others.

Duty: Assigned task.

E

Edit: To revise and prepare for publication.

Endorse: To express approval of; to countersign.

Ensure: To make safe or certain. See *Assure.*

Establish: To set up or bring into existence on a firm basis.

Evaluate: To ascertain or determine the value of.

Examine: To investigate; to scrutinize; to subject to inquiry by inspection or test.

Execute: To put into effect; to follow through to the end.

Exercise: To employ actively, as in authority or influence.

Expedite: To accelerate the movement or progress of, to remove obstacles.

F

Facilitate: To make easy or less difficult.

Feed: To supply material to a machine.

Figure: To compute.

File: To lay away papers, etc., arranged in some methodical manner.

Fill in: To enter information on a form.

Find: To locate by search.

Flag: To mark distinctively.

Follow-up: To check the progress of; to see if results are satisfactory.

Formulate: To develop or devise a plan, policy or procedure and, to put it into a systemized statement.

Furnish: To give or supply. See *Provide.*

G

Goal: An objective.

Guidance: Conducting or directing along a course of action.

I

Implement: To put into effect; to execute.

Inform: To instruct; to communicate knowledge.

Initiate: To originate; to introduce for the first time.

Insert: To put or thrust in.

Inspect: To examine carefully for suitability or conformance with standards. See *Check, Control, Examine, Monitor* and *Verify.*

Instruct: To impart knowledge to; to give information or direction to; to show how to do.

Instructions: To furnish with directions; to inform. *Specific*—Precise and detailed directions that closely limit what can be done or how it can be done. *General*—Directions that are merely outlined, hence do not closely limit what can be done or how it can be done.

Intensive: Exhaustive or concentrated.

Interpret: To explain or clarify; to translate; to elucidate.

Interview: To question in order to obtain facts or opinions.

Inventory: A list of items; stock in hand.

Investigate: To study closely and methodically.

Issue: To distribute formally.

Itemize: To set or note down in detail; to set by particulars.

L

Line: To cover the inside surface of; to draw lines on.

List: To itemize.

Locate: To search for and find; to position.

M

Maintain: To keep up to date or current; to keep at a given level or in working condition.

Manage: To control and direct; to guide; to command the efforts of others towards producing a chosen result. See *Supervise*.

Measure: To find the quality or amount of; to ascertain dimension, count, intensity, etc.

Merge: To combine.

Mix: To unite or blend into one group or mass.

Monitor: To observe or check periodically for a specific purpose.

Multiply: To perform the operation of multiplication.

N

Negotiate: To exchange views and proposals with an eye to reaching agreement by sifting possibilities, proposals, and pros and cons.

Non-routine: Irregular or infrequent situations that arise relating to business or official duties. Characteristic of higher-level jobs.

Note: To observe, notice, heed.

Notify: To give notice to; to inform.

O

Objective: A desired result. See *Goal*.

Observe: To perceive, notice, watch.

Obtain: To gain possession of; to acquire.

Open: To enter upon; to spread out; to make accessible.

Operate: To conduct or perform activity.

Organization: Individuals working together in related ways within a specific structure towards a common end.

Organize: To arrange in interdependent parts; to systemize.

Originate: To produce as new; to invent.

Outline: To make a summary of the significant features of a subject.

P

Participate: To take part in.

Perform: To carry out; to accomplish; to execute.

Place: To locate an employee in a job.

Plan: To devise or project a method or course of action.

Policy: A definite course or method of action selected from among alternatives and in light of given conditions, to guide and determine present and future decisions.

Position Description: A document which describes the purpose, scope, duties, responsibilities, authorities and working relationships associated with a position or entity to be occupied and performed by one person.

Position Specification: A document which describes the physical characteristics, knowledge, skill, experience and educational requirements of a person who would be ideally suited to perform a specific job.

Post: To announce by public, written notice; to transfer or carry information from one record to another.

Practise: To work repeatedly to gain skill.

Prepare: To make ready for a special purpose.

Principle: A governing law of conduct; a fundamental belief serving as a responsible guide to action; a basis for policy.

Procedure: A particular way of accomplishing something or of acting; a series of steps followed in a regular, definite order; a standardized practice.

Proceed: To begin or carry out.

Process: To subject to some special treatment; to handle in accordance with prescribed procedures.

Programme: A series of planned steps towards an objective.

Promote: To act so as to increase sales or patronage; to advance someone to a higher level or job.

Propose: To offer for consideration or adoption; to declare an intention.

Provide: To supply for use; to make available; to furnish.

Purchase: To buy or procure.

Purpose: Something set up as an objective or end to be attained; a reason.

R

Rate: To appraise or assess; to give one's opinion of the rank or quality of.

Receive: To take something that is offered or sent.

Recommend: To advise or counsel a course of action or to suggest for adoption a course of action.

Reconstruct: To restore; to construct again.

Record: To register; to make a record of.

Refer: To direct attention to.

Register: To enter in a record or list.

Release: To authorize the publication of, dissemination of.

Remit: To transmit or send money as payment.

Render: To furnish, contribute.

Report: To supply or furnish organized information.

Represent: To act for or in place of; to serve as a counterpart of; to substitute in some capacity for.

Request: To ask for something.

Require: To demand as necessary or essential.

Requisition: A document making a request.

Research: Inquiry into a specific subject from several sources.

Responsibility: The quality or state of being accountable for.

Responsible for: Having caused; accountable for.

Review: To examine usually with intent to approve or dissent; to analyse results in order to give an opinion.

Revise: To change in order to make new, to correct, to improve, or bring up to date.

Route: To prearrange the sending of an item to the location to which it is to be sent.

Routine: Regular procedure, or normal course of business or official duties.

S

Scan: To examine point by point; to scrutinize.

Schedule: To plan a timetable; to set specific times for.

Screen: To examine so as to separate into two or more groups or classes, usually rejecting one or more.

Search: To look over and through for the purpose of finding something.

Secure: To get possession of; to obtain; to make safe.

Select: Chosen from a number of others of a similar kind.

Separate: To set apart from others for special use; to keep apart.

Serve: To hold an office; to act in a capacity; to discharge a duty or function.

Sign: To authorize by affixing one's signature.

Sort: To put in a definite place or rank according to kind, class, etc.

Stack: To pile up.

Standard of Performance: A statement of the conditions that will exist when a job is acceptably done. Whenever possible the elements of the statement include specific reference to quantity, quality, cost and time.

Stimulate: To excite, rouse or spur on.

Study: To consider attentively; to ponder or fix the mind closely upon a subject.

Submit: To present information for another's judgement or decision.

Subtotal: An interim total.

Subtract: To deduct one number from another.

Summarize: To give only the main points.

Supervise: To oversee a work group, leading, guiding or commanding its efforts to produce a chosen result.

Support: To provide service, assistance or supplies to another person or department.

Survey: To ascertain facts regarding conditions or the condition of a situation usually in connection with the gathering of information.

T

Tabulate: To form into a table by listing; to make a listing.

Trace: To record the transfer of an application or document; to copy as a drawing.

Train: To increase skill or knowledge by capable instruction.

Transcribe: To make a typed copy from shorthand notes or dictated record; to write a copy of.

Transpose: To transfer; to change the usual place or order.

U–V–W–X–Y–Z

Underline: To emphasize or identify by drawing a line under the characters or subject.

Verify: To prove to be true or accurate; to confirm or substantiate; to test or check the accuracy of.

References

Ansoff, Igor (1965). *Corporate Strategy*, New York: McGraw-Hill.

Anstey, Edgar (1989). 'Reminiscences for Wartime Army Psychologists', *The Psychologist*, 2, November, pp. 475–78.

Boyle, S., J. Fullerton and R. Wood (1995). 'Do Assessment/ Development Centres Use Optimum Evaluation Procedures? A Survey of Practice in UK Organizations', *International Journal of Selection and Assessment*, 3(2), pp. 132–40.

Bray, D.W. (1964). 'The Assessment Center Method of Appraising Management Potential', in D.W. Blood (ed.), *The Personnel Job in a Changing World*, New York: American Management Association (AMA).

Burgoyne, J.G. and R. Stuart (1976). 'The Nature, Use and Acquisition of Managerial Skills and Other Attributes', *Personnel Review*, 5(4), pp. 19–29.

Chanda, A. and S. Kabra (2000). *Human Resource Strategy- Architecture for Change*, New Delhi: Response Books.

Clifford, L. and H. Bennett (1997). 'Best Practice in 360-degree Feedback', *Selection and Development Review*, April.

Cooper, Kenneth Carlton (2000). *Effective Competency Modeling and Reporting*, New York: AMA Publications.

Davis, R.S. and D.A. Olson (1996–97). 'Leverage Training and Development to Make a Strategic Impact', *The Journal* (Society of Insurance Trainers and Educators), pp. 10–12.

Dubois, D. (1993). *Competency Based Performance Improvement, A Strategy for Organisational Change*, Amherst, Mass.: HRD Press.

Dulewicz, V. and C.A. Fletcher (1982). 'The Relationship between Previous Experience, Intelligence and Background Characteristics of Participants and their Performance in an Assessment Center', *Journal of Occupational Psychology*, 55(3).

Eisenberg, Andrea (1999). *Public Communication*, January.

Eubanks, J.L., J.B. Marshal and M.P. O'Driscoll (1990). 'A Competency Model for OD Practitioners', *Training and Development Journal*, November, pp. 85–90.

Finkle, R.B. (1976). 'Managerial Assessment Centers', in M.D. Dunnette (ed.), *Handbook of Industrial Organizational Psychology*, Chicago, IL: Rand-McNally, pp. 861–88.

Flanagan, J.C. (1954). 'The Critical Incident Technique', *Psychological Bulletin*, 51(4), pp. 327–58.

Fletcher, C.A. and V. Dulewicz (1984). 'An Empirical Study of a UK-based Assessment Center', *Journal of Management Studies*, 21(1).

Gluck, W.F. and L.R. Jauch (1984). *Strategic Management and Business Policy*, New York: McGraw-Hill.

Hamel, Gary and C.K. Prahalad (1994). *Competing for the Future*, Boston: Harvard Business School.

Hayes, Robert H. (1985). 'Strategic Planning—Forward in Reverse?', *Harvard Business Review*, November–December, pp. 111–19.

Hogg, B. (1993). 'European Managerial Competencies', *European Business Review*, 93(2), pp. 21–26.

Holdeman, J.B., J.M. Aldridge and D. Jackson (1996). 'How to Hire Ms/Mr Right?', *Journal of Accountancy*, August, pp. 55–57.

Kelly, G.A. (1955). *The Psychology of Personal Constructs* (Vols I & II), New York: Norten.

Klemp, G.O. (ed.) (1980). *The Assessment of Occupational Competence*, Washington, DC, Report to the National Institution of Education.

Linkage, Inc. (1997). *Introduction to Competency Modeling*, Lexington, Mass.: Linkage.

Lowry, P.E. (1996). 'A Survey of the Assessment Centre Process in the Public Sector', *Public Personnel Management*, 25(3), pp. 307–21.

Mabey, W. (1989). 'The Majority of Large Companies Use Occupational Tests', *Guidance and Assessment Review*, 5(3), pp. 1–4.

MacKinnon, D.W. (1977). 'From Selecting Spies to Selecting Managers: The OSS Assessment Program', in J.L. Moses and W.C. Byham (eds), *Applying the Assessment Center Method*, New York: Pergamon.

McClelland, David C. (1973). 'Testing for Competency Rather than Intelligence', *American Psychologist*, 28, January, pp. 1–14.

McIlvaine, A.R. (1998). 'World Premiere', *Human Resource Executive*, 19, October, pp. 18–20.

McLagan, P.A. (1989). *The Models of HRD Practice*, Alexandria, VA: American Society for Training and Development.

Parry, S.R. (1996). 'The Quest for Competencies', *Training*, July, pp. 48–56.

Porter, Michael E. (1982). 'Industrial Organization and the Evaluation of Concepts for Strategic Planning', in T.H. Naylor (ed.), *Corporate Strategic*. New York.

Roberton and Makin (1994). 'Discourse and Agency—The Example of Personal Psychology and "Assessment Centre"', *Organization Studies*, Mid Winter. Available at http://findarticles.com/p/articles/mi_m4339/is_n6_v15/ai_16736641/pg_4

Selgnick, Philips (1957). *Leadership in Administration*, New York: Harper.

Spencer, Legde M. and Sigme M. Spencer (1993). *Competence at Work*, New York: John Wiley & Sons Inc.

Taylor, Frederick W. (1911). *Principles of Scientific Management*, New York: Harper.

Index

About the Author

Seema Sanghi is a well-known consultant and trainer with over 21 years of experience in the field of organizational behaviour and psychometric assessment. Recipient of the Mother Teresa Award, three gold medals and numerous merit scholarships, she is at present Managing Director, STYRAX Consultancy Pvt Ltd and is former Director, FORE School of Management, New Delhi. She obtained her doctorate in Organizational Psychology from the University of Rajasthan.

Professor Sanghi has developed and published over 80 psychometric tests and a number of research publications. She is an expert in the development of tools, competency mapping, assessment centres, personality profiling and organizational surveys. She has undertaken major consultancy assignments of both the public and private sectors. She has also organized management development programmes in customer care, team building, managerial effectiveness, leader-ship, communication, mentoring and other soft skills. Her recent research has been in the areas of cross-cultural management and ethical issues. She has also published *The Handbook of Competency Mapping: Understanding, Designing and Implementing Competency Models in Organizations* (2004) and her best-selling book *Organizational Behaviour* (2005), co-authored with Stephens P. Robbins and Timothy A. Judge, has been appreciated by the former president Dr A.P.J. Abdul Kalam.

Seema Sanghi is Director and Chair Professor (Organisational Behaviour and Human Resources) at FORE School of Management, New Delhi.